# Gender, genre
# and the Romantic poets

# Gender, genre and the Romantic poets

## An introduction

PHILIP COX

Manchester University Press

Manchester and New York

distributed exclusively in the USA and Canada by St. Martin's Press

Copyright © Philip Cox 1996

*Published by* Manchester University Press
Oxford Road, Manchester M13 9NR, UK
*and* Room 400, 175 Fifth Avenue, New York, NY 10010, USA

*Distributed exclusively in the USA and Canada*
*by* St. Martin's Press, Inc., 175 Fifth Avenue, New York, NY 10010, USA

*British Library Cataloguing-in-Publication Data*
A catalogue record is available from the British Library

*Library of Congress Cataloging-in-Publication Data*
Cox, Philip.
    Gender, genre and the Romantic poets : an introduction / Philip Cox.
        p.    cm.
    Includes bibliographical references (p.    ).
    ISBN 0–7190–4263–1. — ISBN 0–7190–4264–X (alk. paper)
    1. English poetry—19th century—History and criticism.    2. Sex
(Psychology) in literature.    3. Romanticism—Great Britain.
4. Literary form.    5. e-uk.    I. Title.
PR590.C64    1996
821'.809353—dc20                                                          95–41314

ISBN 0 7190 4263 1 *hardback*
        0 7190 4264 X *paperback*

*First published* 1996
00 99 98 97 96        10 9 8 7 6 5 4 3 2 1

Typeset in Great Britain
by Northern Phototypesetting Co Ltd, Bolton
Printed in Great Britain
by Bell & Bain Limited, Glasgow

# Contents

# Acknowledgements

I wish to thank the Cultural Research Institute at Sheffield Hallam University for the sabbatical leave which enabled me to work uninterruptedly on a large section of this book. I also wish to thank my colleagues in the English department for their support and encouragement, particularly Robert Miles who has followed the progress of my work from its very earliest stages, offering advice and well-informed criticism. My many discussions with Julie Morrissy have made a considerable and invaluable contribution to the final book. Thanks are due to the staff at the Mary Badland Library of Sheffield Hallam University and to Anita Roy of Manchester University Press who has had faith in this project from the beginning.

Much earlier versions of parts of Chapter 1 appeared in Horst Höhne (ed.), *Romantic Discourses* and *The Journal of Gender Studies*; an earlier version of Chapter 4 appeared in *The Keats–Shelley Journal*. I thank the respective editors for their permission to repeat material here.

Bakewell
1995
P.C.

# Introduction

## I

Throughout the twentieth century, literary critics writing about the 'Romantic Poets', or 'Romanticism' in general, have been forced to recognise the extremely problematic nature of their critical project. Marilyn Butler usefully reminds us that our attempts to define the concept of Romanticism are themselves influenced by different attitudes towards the very form and function of literary history itself. She observes that:

Twentieth-century notions of Romanticism are fed by two intellectual traditions. One tradition tries to understand Romanticism aesthetically, as a theory about the nature and origin of art. The other attempts to see it as a historical phenomenon which must be associated with political and social circumstances. The problem, however, is that these approaches are not independent of one another.[1]

On the one hand, critics have attempted to define certain theories about poetry and art as 'Romantic', thus creating an aesthetic category which can be applied to a work of art from any period. In this way, for example, a novel such as Emily Bronte's *Wuthering Heights*, which was not published until 1847, can be read as an essentially 'Romantic' text alongside those produced by writers working fifty or more years earlier.[2] On the other hand, there has been a tendency to define Romanticism in terms of a specific historical period, in which certain 'Romantic' ideas were developed, and to relate this development to a range of cultural, social and political contexts, particularly those provided by the French Revolution and British responses to it. As Butler points out, however, these two approaches to Romanticism are inevitably interconnected because the general aesthetic category of 'Romanticism' is seen to have its intellectual roots in a distinct historical period. This in turn leads to further problems, particularly those connected with the validity of applying a historically precise phenomenon to the literary texts of a later period which inevitably possesses its own, significantly different, cultural determinants.

The general dilemma outlined by Butler has resulted in the common critical usage of two separate but inevitably related terms, namely 'Romanticism' and 'the Romantic Period'. The term 'Romanticism' has been used to refer to a general aesthetic category, whilst the 'Romantic Period' refers to that literary period in Britain which spans the late eighteenth and early nineteenth centuries, during which time, it is argued, 'Romantic' ideas first gained their currency. However, this further distinction creates further problems, for to describe a particular literary period as 'Romantic' assumes a certain uniformity in terms of its literary interests and output; and, as anyone who has even only just begun to study the period well knows, this is far from being the case. The American critic Jerome McGann has, as a result of this, argued for the need for us to be aware of the critical constructs through which we have come to view late eighteenth- and early nineteenth-century literature. In an overview of his (considerable) contribution to the debate over the definition of 'Romanticism', he recalls how he has

worked hard to clarify the distinction between 'the romantic period' (that is, a particular historical epoch) and 'romanticism' (that is, a set of cultural/ideological formations that came to prominence during the romantic period). The distinction is important not merely because so much of the work of that period is not 'romantic', but even more, perhaps, because the period is notable for its many ideological struggles. A romantic ethos achieved dominance through sharp cultural conflict; some of the fiercest engagements were internecine – the civil wars of the romantic movement itself.[3]

McGann suggests the extent to which the texts we label as 'Romantic' diverge from one another and, indeed, enter into ideological conflict with one another. As the chapters which follow will demonstrate, the 'Romantic Poets' share as many dissimilarities as similarities. However, perhaps even more relevant to our immediate concerns is McGann's earlier observation that a large amount of the work produced during the Romantic Period is not 'romantic'. This, as much as anything, calls into question the relevance of the historical category, for we must ask to what extent the term 'the Romantic Period' is a misrepresentation of the literary output of the period as a whole.

Recent work on the limits and limitations of the Romantic canon, particularly work done on women's writing of the period (as will be seen), has brought this problem of misrepresentation more prominently to the fore. Having said this, it has nearly always been the case that literary critics have alerted their readers to the diversity within Romanticism and the Romantic Period. None the less, such claims for diversity have often been associated with a narrowness of critical focus. M.H. Abrams, for example, in his seminal essay from 1963 entitled 'English Romanticism: The Spirit of the Age', notes that 'Romanticism is no one thing. It is many very individual poets, who wrote poems manifesting a greater diversity of qualities, it seems to me, than those of any preceding age.'[4] Whilst recognising diversity here, Abrams contains such diversity within the single category of 'Romanticism': rather than Romanticism being one element within a diverse range of writings, it becomes the central defining term of its own inner diversity. Whilst he makes a claim for the unrivalled range of Romanticism, Abrams at the same time limits its application, most obviously in terms of genre – Romanticism is equated solely with poetry, any other genre is tacitly excluded from consideration. This tendency is made particularly worrying by the way in which the critic slips effortlessly within two sentences from talking of 'Romanticism' as an aesthetic category to a discussion of a Romantic 'age' in a way which conflates the two categories which McGann and others have subsequently teased apart.

Like the Romantic poets of whom he writes, Abrams is ultimately concerned with the quest for an ultimate unity in the diversity he observes. As the essay continues he notes that

some prominent qualities a number of these poems share, and certain of these shared qualities form a distinctive complex which may, with a high degree of probability, be related to the events and ideas of the cataclysmic coming-into-being of the world to which we are by now becoming fairly accustomed.[5]

Out of the diversity Abrams delineates a unified 'distinctive complex' from the evidence of 'a number of these poems' and then proceeds to define his 'age' according to the criteria thus established. In perhaps his most influential, important and intellectually stimulating book, *The Mirror and the Lamp: Romantic Theory and the Critical Tradition* (1958), Abrams essentially defines Romanticism by focusing his attention upon the self-definitions of a small group of poets (the 'Big Six': Blake, Coleridge, Wordsworth, Keats, Shelley and, to a lesser extent, Byron) who are always already defined by the academy as 'Romantic'. Abrams effectively colludes with the poets' own self-definitions of themselves as representative of their age; he pays belated acknowledgement to their self-promoted status, which was largely unacknowledged by their contemporaries, as poetic and cultural legislators.

In the last quotation from Abrams's essay it can be seen how he associates the Romantic Period with the coming-into-being of the period in which the critic himself lives. There is a sense of the critic being crucially involved with the 'age' and its writings which he is in the process of discussing. Arden Reed, in his introduction to *Romanticism and Language* (1984), relates this tendency in what one might term 'traditional' Romantic criticism to a shared 'ideological response' between poets and critics. American critics of the 1920s and 1930s, he argues, were generally hostile to the study of the Romantic poets whom they saw as producing work which was 'slack, sloppy and vague'. In defending their chosen poets against such charges, Arden suggests, scholars of Romanticism echoed the poets' own defences. He notes that:

This ideological strain should have been predictable because it was already operating among the Romantics themselves, nowhere more so than in Coleridge's criticism, from which the modern apologists largely took their lead. In such passages as Chapter 14 of *Biographia Literaria* Coleridge formulated what M.H. Abrams in *The Mirror and the Lamp* called the Romantics' distinctive contribution to aesthetic theory – the idea that the imagination is a creative faculty, the locus of genius and the source of originality (all highly problematic terms that critics rarely questioned, at least in a self-conscious way).[6]

The Romantic poets and their twentieth-century critics, suggests Reed, share certain 'ideological' beliefs and both stress the centrality of such self-defining Romantic categories as the creative imagination, poetic genius and the importance of originality. Moreover, in this (non-)critical act of mirroring their predecessors, the twentieth-century critics of Romanticism forsake both a 'self-conscious' approach to their own methodology and a distinct critical position from which to view the work of the Romantic poets themselves.

In response to this double dilemma, Reed and others (most notably Paul de Man and his followers) turned to the deconstructive theories of Jacques Derrida as a means to gain critical self-awareness and a leverage upon the self-defining nature of Romanticism:

deconstruction offers a way to interrogate the ideologies by which earlier critics had underwritten Romanticism while still allowing for, if not encouraging, a sustained reading of that literature ... deconstruction underlines, for instance, difference and intertextuality, and thus enables readings of texts that stage no reconciliations.[7]

If 'traditional' Romantic criticism had suggested that Romantic poetry had an essentially self-defining coherence, deconstructive criticism offered the opportunity for critics to explore the gaps and fissures within the poems they read. Romantic poetry increasingly came to be seen as concerned with its own self-contradictions, and its own lack of closure or 'reconciliation' was often mirrored by the critic's own inventive playfulness.[8] My own approach within the present book owes much to a methodology derived from deconstructive insights, particularly those offered by the work of Derrida. However, I also work with an awareness of what Stephen Copley and John Whale have called deconstruction's 'ambiguous, even collusive relationship with the literary'.[9] This 'collusion' can take many forms and it is relevant here just to gesture towards two areas in which a narrowly deconstructive approach reveals its inadequacies. Firstly, deconstructive criticism frequently works from an unproblematic assumption of the canonical status of the Romantic poets. Whilst the textual complexities of the Big Six are subjected to rigorous analysis, the reasons behind the choice of text being analysed remain unspoken. Whilst the idiosyncratic American critic Harold Bloom is hardly a representative figure, it seems none the less fitting that as one of the editors and contributors to *Deconstruction and Criticism* (1979) he should more recently have published *The Western Canon* (1995) in which he presents a passionate and controversially conservative defence of the traditional canons of western literature. Bloom is, of course, perhaps best known for his theory of the 'anxiety' of poetic influence, a theory based upon an oedipal male competitiveness which at the same time pays heed to deconstruction's 'intertextual' interests as identified by Arden Reed. In Chapter 3 I engage with the consequences of such male-centred approaches to intertextuality.

If deconstruction has offered critics the means by which to gain leverage upon the self-reflexive tendencies of more traditional Romantic criticism, then similar possibilities have also been provided by a very different methodology, that of the various 'new' historicisms. The return to history in Romantic criticism has perhaps been most eloquently championed by Jerome McGann. McGann, like

Reed, writes in opposition to the unvoiced assumptions of critics such as Abrams:

Abrams offers a program of Romanticism rather than a critical representation of its character; as such [he reifies] certain key Romantic self-conceptualizations like 'spirituality', 'creativity', 'process', 'uniqueness', 'diversity'. Indeed, the concepts of 'synthesis' and 'reconciliation' as these appear in the received Romantic texts and their commentaries are themselves Romantic concepts whose meaning cannot be taken at face value. They lie at the very heart of Romanticism's self-representation and as such they must be subjected to critical analysis. This analysis is difficult to perform, however, since the ideologies of Romanticism seek to persuade us that such concepts are fundamental, and hence that they need not – cannot – be analysed.[10]

Taking his cue from the work of the German nineteenth-century writer Heinrich Heine, McGann suggests that the only way for us to break free from this 'Romantic Ideology' is to adopt a 'double vision which asks the critic to call into question those representations which a cultural subject offers as an explanation of itself'.[11] For McGann, and others, this 'double vision' is attained by an awareness of history, of the ways in which poetic texts are produced by certain historical conditions in which they perform specific ideological functions. He returns to the self-defining aspects of Romanticism noted by Reed but, rather than deconstructing their apparent internal cogency, he exposes it to the vicissitudes of historical process:

When reading Romantic poems, then, we are to remember that their ideas – for example, ideas about the creativity of Imagination, about the centrality of the Self, about the organic and processive structure of natural and social life, and so forth – are all historically specific in a crucial and paradoxical sense ... In the Romantic Age these and similar ideas are represented as trans-historical – eternal truths which wake to perish never. The very belief that transcendental categories can provide a permanent ground for culture becomes, in the Romantic Age, an ideological formation – another illusion raised up to hold back an awareness of the contradictions inherent in contemporary social structures and the relations they support.[12]

I have said that my approach in this book owes much to deconstructive methodologies in that I am particularly interested in looking at the ways in which the poems I analyse reveal a variety of telling gaps and indeterminacies which subvert the possibility of textual closure. Having said this, my interest in such moments of indeterminacy is guided by what they can tell us about the text's relationship with the 'contradictions' within the 'contemporary social structures' to which a historicist criticism alerts us.

The particular social structures I am interested in are those which relate to issues of gender in the late eighteenth and early nineteenth centuries but, more than this, I am interested in the connections between such issues and the deployment of certain literary genres within that period. This inevitably brings us back to a reconsideration of the Romantic canon, for, as I mentioned earlier, recent scholarly research, particularly by feminist critics, has called into question the representative nature of a canon which, essentially, contains only six poets, all of them male.[13] As Sandra Gilbert and Susan Gubar, amongst others, point out, the interpretative 'narrative' which has been constructed to read these male poets has inevitably been a masculinist one. They cite, for example, the introductory essay on 'Romantic Poetry' by Harold Bloom and Lionel Trilling in the *Oxford Anthology of English Literature* (1973) in which the 'narrative' of Romantic poetry is seen as analogous to a male quest: 'Quest becomes the journey to re-beget the self, to be one's father, and the pattern of the poetic career assumes the shapes of the life cycle of what we now call Freudian or Psychological Man.'[14] The masculine, self-engendering nature of this narrative is one which self-evidently excludes both femininity and women, and subsequent challenges to the Romantic canon have stressed that there are many extra-canonical texts from the same historical period which relate different stories. As Anne Mellor puts it in her introduction to *Romanticism and Feminism* (1988):

In the future, a feminist as well as a new historical criticism of the Romantic period must challenge these traditional prejudices and undertake the intellectual enquiry already well underway in other fields of English and American literary criticism, the opening and reshaping of the literary canon. We must read with renewed attention and appreciation the hundreds of female and male writers working in the early nineteenth century, all those novelists, essayists, journalists, diarists, and letter-writers who had narratives to tell other than those plotted as 'natural supernaturalism' or 'the romantic sublime' or 'romantic irony'.[15]

Since Mellor wrote this, such work has been undertaken by a large number of critics and many of these newly recovered narratives are being re-told after years of neglect. What is striking, however, is that the narrative of Romanticism, as a narrative, refuses to go away: its grand claims for its own importance might now appear to be a misrepresentation of the material evidence but it none the less remains true to say that the power of Romanticism's self-defining presence still retains a force. Stephen Copley and John Whale note how '[t]hose marginalized figures standing outside the Romantic canon are there precisely because of the excluding power of the prevailing narratives'.[16] This is not, of course, to say that we should accept the 'Romantic Ideology' and collude with this 'excluding power'. It does, however, suggest that the power of the Romantic canon still deserves – indeed requires – critical analysis as a specific cultural phenomenon in its own right. As Susan Wolfson puts it:

> insofar as the set of epistemic, discursive, and political concerns most aptly described as 'Romanticism' are sufficiently and significantly different from what characterizes the wider contemporaneous literary culture, the 'Romantic' canon must remain select and exclusive of other discourses, whether those of women's writing or, in another perspective, genres beyond the ones that have defined this canon and its place in subsequent literary history and culture.[17]

She proceeds to suggest that perhaps such exclusivity might lead to the obsolescence of 'Romanticism' as a useful critical term or (and I think this is more likely) to the demotion of Romanticism to a 'relative phenomenon' within a broader understanding of the period's literature. For the present, however, I would argue that the study of the canonical texts of Romanticism, which, as we have noticed, have continued to exert a powerful influence upon twentieth-century critics, can lead us to an understanding of the disturbed and unsettled nature of masculinity in the late eighteenth and early nineteenth centuries. Approaching the poetry with the 'double vision' advocated by McGann, we can begin to see how, to use the words of Pierre Macherey, 'the text explores ideology' and provides it with a 'visible and determinate form' which allows its workings to be revealed.[18]

  In one of the quotations from M.H. Abrams it was seen how, in terms of a broad generic category, Romanticism was effectively defined in terms of poetry and it is still generally the case that the Romantic canon is almost exclusively poetic, as Wolfson also implies. When the relationship between gender and genre in this period is considered it is also often thought of in these broad generic terms: male writers are associated with poetry and female writers with the novel. An early formulation of this view is provided in an essay by Irene Taylor and Gina Luria who note that the high claims made for poetry effectively excluded women from being taken seriously as poets:

The novel, of course, had none of those high-flown claims as genre that would make it inaccessible to female writers; indeed women had always been stigmatized as novel readers; what more logical than that they should in turn provide this feminized food for their own audience? The surprise is that they managed to develop through the genre a new dignity both for it and themselves.[19]

Whilst one could cite evidence to support this view of the relationship between gender and genre, particularly in the earlier part of the period, it represents none the less a simplification of literary history.[20] More recent research has shown that, in this instance as in others, the so-called Romantic period was a period of transition. Towards the end of the period, more men were beginning to write novels (perhaps the example of Sir Walter Scott is important here) and, more significantly for the present argument, more women were writing poetry. As the subtitle of Marlon B. Ross's important book *The Contours of Masculine Desire: Romanticism and the Rise of Women's Poetry* (1989) makes clear, the 'Romantic Period' and, perhaps ironically, 'Romanticism', were clearly associated with the emergence of a distinctive line of poetry by female poets. Yet, as more women became poets (and as poetry itself thus came to be seen as increasingly feminised), the genre of poetry began to lose its cultural dominance. Stuart Curran wryly remarks that 'It is probably true that the role of the poetess was a trap enforced by masculine disdain for cultural refinement and that just as women became known as the principal poets of England the novel was reappropriated by men and made the dominant genre.'[21] For the male poet writing at this time in a feminized genre, therefore, the question of his own masculinity assumed an ever more important role, particularly in light of Romantic poetry's focus upon the 'self' which was, in itself, a product of the same situation. Given this dilemma which exists at the heart of Romantic poetry, my aim in this book is to explore not the broad generic opposition between the novel and poetry but the sub-genres at play within poetry itself. Little critical attention has been given to the ways in which different poetic genres (such as the pastoral, the sonnet, the ode, the epic and the verse drama – to name but a few of

the genres discussed in the pages that follow) are intricately connected with a discourse of gender difference. Anne Mellor has noted
how '[a]ny writer, male or female, could occupy the "masculine" or
"feminine" ideological or subject position, even within the same
work', and it is my intention to illustrate how an attention to the
poet's use of generic conventions can alert us to the shifting – and
often conflicting – gender positions within the poetry.[22] Through
such analysis it is possible to move towards a clearer understanding
of how poetic genre works within specific texts, how such generic
usage can both collude with and challenge traditional gender boundaries, and, finally, how the poetry of the canonical male Romantic
poets relates to contemporary notions of masculinity and femininity.

## II

In approaching the subject of literary genre and its relationship to
wider cultural and ideological oppositions, it is useful to turn to
Jacques Derrida's important essay 'The Law of Genre'. In this essay,
Derrida begins by stressing the apparently dogmatic and repressive
element that the notion and presence of genre, both in a text and in
the absract, appear to invoke: 'As soon as the word genre is sounded,
as soon as it is heard, as soon as one attempts to conceive it, a limit
is drawn. And when a limit is established, norms and interdictions
are not far behind.'[23] This would seem to respond to our instinctive
sense of how genre functions, for we tend to think immediately of
rules and restrictions when we consider the role played by a specific
genre or genres within a specific literary work. Moreover, Derrida's
discussion of 'norms and interdictions' might make us think of the
particular difficulties to be faced in a study of the role of genre in
Romantic poetry – poetry created by poets who often expressed a
belief in the uniqueness of the individual work of art; poetry which
often apparently attempted to defy the established 'norms and interdictions' of the society which produced it. Stuart Curran has demonstrated the use made by the Romantic poets of traditional poetic
forms but the emphasis in his study is none the less often upon the
redeployment and imaginative reworking of such literary 'norms'.
Indeed, Curran lists some of the most interesting Romantic poems
under the category-defying category of 'composite orders'.[24]

However, this mode of approach to the question of genre is somewhat complicated by the central and most radical contention within

Derrida's essay. Derrida makes the apparently simple point that all texts must contain a 'mark' which announces that they belong to a certain genre and that they are to be aligned with the previous texts that have been grouped within a specific generic category. The startling turn in the essay emerges with the observation that this 'mark' cannot itself be part of the genre which it announces, for it speaks from outside of the genre and directs attention to something other than itself. Thus, to take a reasonably self-evident example (that will also be of relevance in the next chapter), a 'pastoral' poem often declares itself to be 'A Pastoral Poem' and yet this act of generic self-declaration, which provides a framework within which the poem is to be read, necessarily exists outside of the 'pastoral' discourse of the rest of the poem. In announcing adherence to a certain genre, therefore, the 'mark' also announces its difference, its otherness. As Derrida puts it: 'In marking itself generically, a text unmarks itself [se demarque] ... The clause or floodgate of genre declasses what it allows to be classed. It tolls the knell of genealogy or of genericity, which it however also brings forth to the light of day.'[25] In this sense, then, genre and the law of genre are always undermining or, to use a more apposite word, deconstructing themselves. Rather than the strict law of 'norms and interdictions' which we habitually think of in relation to genre, Derrida presents a generic theory which is dependent upon a 'principle of contamination': 'It is precisely a principle of contamination, a law of impurity, a parasitical economy. In the code of set theories, if I may use it at least figuratively, I would speak of a certain participation without belonging – a taking part in without being part of, without having membership in a set.'[26] From this perspective, then, our traditional view of the Romantics' use of genre as radically challenging has to be modified by our sense of the issue of genre itself being radically challenged.

In terms of my own concerns, Derrida's essay is particularly interesting because it works within a very broad definition of the notion of 'genre'. He observes that:

The question of the literary genre is not a formal one: it covers the motif of the law in general, of generation in the natural and symbolic senses, of birth in the natural and symbolic senses, of the generation of difference, sexual difference between the masculine and feminine gender, of the hymen between the two, of a relationless relation between the two, of an identity and difference between the feminine and the masculine.[27]

There are a variety of ways in which one could explore the relationship between gender and genre (the word *genre* applying, of course, to both in the French language) but Derrida directs us to fundamental processes of categorisation and implies that radical uncertainties in one area of discourse can be related to manifest uncertainties in others.

It is this aspect of Derrida's thought which has evidently been of use to recent feminist theory – for example, that found in the work of Hélène Cixous. In 'Sorties' Cixous argues that all discourse is structured in terms of binary oppositions which ultimately relate to the opposition between the social constructs of masculinity and femininity.[28] Crucially, these binary oppositions, she claims, are always 'hierarchized oppositions', oppositions which are finally destructive and life-denying:

Theory of culture, theory of society, the ensemble of symbolic systems – art, religion, family, language, – everything elaborates the same systems. And the movement by which each opposition is set up to produce meaning is the movement by which the couple is destroyed. A universal battlefield. Each time a war breaks out. Death is always at work.[29]

Cixous thus implicitly converts Derrida's more general (and perhaps more apolitical) theory into a specifically feminist political tool. In following the leads of Derrida and Cixous, then, our consideration of the Romantic use of genre should be aware of the innate instabilities within the 'law of genre' itself and also of how those instabilities relate to a wider discursive field than that which is normally designated as the 'literary'. Following Cixous in particular, one might want to trace the ways in which generic tensions rehearse the struggles, inequalities and uncertainties of gender and reveal the instabilities inherent in what is apparently the essentially masculine ideology of Romanticism.

My purpose in offering this deconstructive–feminist framework for the analysis which follows in subsequent chapters is to emphasise from the outset my belief that the socially constructed categories of masculinity and femininity are neither fixed binary oppositions nor are they tied to biological sexual difference. Throughout this book it will be seen how male Romantic writers adopt subject positions within their work which, according to contemporary criteria, would have been judged as 'feminine'. The relationship between male writers and both masculinity and femininity is therefore a complex one and one that needs to be negotiated with great care. My discussion of Keats in Chapter 4, for example, develops an understanding of what was seen by his peers as the writer's poetical 'effeminacy'. Such effeminacy shares certain qualities with the feminine, and Keats can in a variety of different ways be read as a poet who adopts a feminine subject position within his work in an attempt to challenge cultural constructions of masculinity. However, it is also the case that such 'effeminacy' can be read in relation to cultural and economic forces that have their origins in the large social changes that took place during the eighteenth century. G.J. Barker-Benfield notes that during this period:

Male writers recognised the large changes commercial capitalism was bringing in Britain and tended increasingly to advocate them as signs of the progress of civilization. Yet they had profound doubts, concerned as they were with the effects on hierarchy should everyone freely pursue worldly pleasure. A persistent and fundamental concern was the meaning of changed manners for manhood, traditionally bound up with classical and warrior ideals. The 'degeneracy' to which the rise of the 'monied interest' and the decline of the citizen soldier was believed to lead had a gender-specific dimension, expressed in the widespread use of the term, 'effeminacy.'[30]

This 'gender-specific' aspect of cultural response to economic change can be traced in the ways in which contemporary critics of Keats's work conflated his middle-class social status with what they described as his poetical 'effeminacy'. The perceived transgressions of class barriers were in effect being read in terms of a transgressive deployment of gender difference. A similar matrix of economic and gender issues is to be found in Coleridge's 'Reflections on having left a Place of Retirement' (which I discuss in Chapter 1) where the poet's ambiguous response to commerce is revealed through an ambivalently gendered treatment of the concept of 'Luxury'.[31]

In reading the work of the male Romantic poets in terms of 'masculinity' and 'femininity', therefore, we must be aware of the complex cultural nuances of the gendered subject positions they adopt. Of crucial importance is the fact that the adoption of a feminine role by a man is inevitably read differently by society from the adoption of such a role by a woman: society either measures the man's performance against its expectations of a 'suitable' masculinity or looks for signs of such masculinity through the performed femininity. Judith Still and Michael Worton note the 'long tradition of "effeminate" men' which includes 'Elizabethan courtiers, fops, exquisites, beaux' and 'dandies' and proceed to observe that

its main importance lies less in its appropriation of femininity than in its theatricality, in its performativity and consequent non-referentiality. There must always be a political subtext to extravagant (or, conversely, minimalist) visual ornamentation or to cross-dressing. However, we would point out that the adoption by men of 'feminine' dress codes is usually determined and accompanied by a concern with display, with the ways in which aesthetic – and ultimately, ontological – beliefs can be proclaimed by the ways in which the body is dressed and presented for public scrutiny. Displays and paradings by men of effeminacy need not, of course, entail a loss of masculinity.[32]

Although Still and Worton are specifically discussing dress codes here, one can apply their observations metaphorically to the performance of different gendered subject positions within a literary text. Their starting point is the assumption that, as performance, there is no direct referentiality between gender and biological sex. Thus a man who acts (or writes) in a way that will be interpreted as feminine deliberately highlights the discrepancy between his maleness and his actions in order to convey an ultimately 'political' message. One might want to argue, therefore, that Keats's effeminacy cannot be reduced simply to femininity but needs to be read as a separate category, that of the feminine as self-consciously performed by a male (whose own masculinity is not, perhaps, finally usurped). I would want to argue none the less for the positive and constructive aspects of such performance. Central to recent developments in this area of gender studies has been the work of Judith Butler who, noting the discontinuity between biological sex difference and social constructions of gender, observes that

if gender is instituted through acts which are internally discontinuous, then the *appearance of substance* is precisely that, a constructed identity, a performative accomplishment which the mundane social audience, including the actors themselves, come to believe and to perform in the mode of belief.[33]

The deliberate performance of the 'wrong' identity that metaphorical cross-dressing involves works to subvert the 'mode of belief' which clings unthinkingly to certain gender expectations. In this way the adoption or performance of feminine subject positions by male poets can be read as possessing a positively deconstructive force and a potentially powerful political subtext (even if, as will be seen, there is often textual resistance to the implications of this subversive potential).

## III

The first chapter of this book enlarges upon many of the observations made in this brief introduction by focusing upon a specific genre, pastoral, and two short poems, Samuel Taylor Coleridge's 'Reflections on having left a Place of Retirement' and Anna Laetitia Barbauld's 'To Mr. C – – – GE', which relate not only to the genre in question but to one another. Drawing upon Jacques Derrida's theoretical approach to generic categorisation, and using the work of Hélène Cixous to describe the gender implications of such categories, I illustrate some of the ways in which discourses of gender are intimately involved with other discourses of the period. At the same time, my analysis of the poem by Barbauld helps to indicate the particular problems that women poets experienced in situating themselves within a literary practice which was, in the 1790s, still effectively gendered as masculine.

The first of my two chapters on William Wordsworth develops the observations made in the discussion of Coleridge and Barbauld in two ways: firstly, by examining the gender implications of Wordsworth's use of the sonnet form and, secondly, by exploring the generic relationship between the sonnet and the ode. Genres, like any other signs within a semantic system, cannot function independently and, by paying particular attention to the generic indeterminacy of 'Tintern Abbey', I show how the instabilities of the poem reflect an uncertainty concerning the masculine self and the romantic imagination. In both chapters on Wordsworth I make frequent use of theoretical frameworks derived from the writings of Julia Kristeva, whose accounts of the very first emergence of a sense of 'self' within the child provide a useful interpretative tool for the exploration of the Romantic poets' treatment of the same theme and which are also particularly helpful in alerting us to the gendered aspects of such self-creation. Moreover, Kristeva's emphasis upon the importance of the mother–child relationship for the formation of the 'self' offers a way of challenging the male-centred Oedipal narrative of Romanticism presented by Harold Bloom and others. In my use of Kristeva's synthesis of psychoanalytic and cultural critique, I am building upon the work of other feminist critics of Romanticism during the past ten years, particularly that of Mary Jacobus on *The Prelude*.[34]

The second chapter on Wordsworth is perhaps more ambitious than the preceding chapters, and this is no doubt linked to that fact that its subject is one of the most ambitious of all Romantic poems – *The Prelude*. As an epic, Wordsworth's long autobiographical poem represents what is traditionally perceived as the most elevated of literary genres, one which is also, to a significant extent, a composite form which subsumes all other genres within its vast ambition. In dealing with such a poem it is inevitable that the issue of literary influence and precedence should come to the fore, although it is clear that problems pertaining to the relationship between a specific poem and poetic tradition are an important part of any study concerned with genre. In dealing with the issue of poetic influence, I draw out the gender implications of such interactions between living and dead poets and, in doing this, I suggest ways in which Harold Bloom's notion of a masculine 'anxiety of influence' might be replaced by an implicitly feminine alternative – although it remains debatable whether Wordsworth's own poem ultimately subscribes to this kind of femininity (which inevitably presents a challenge to his own poetic identity).

Both Coleridge and Wordsworth, despite the interesting oscillations and ambiguities which can be detected within their work, construct essentially masculine versions of the self within their poetry: with John Keats this would appear to be different. Keats, famously in his description of the desired state of 'negative capability', frequently offers his readers a version of the poet who is apparently gendered as feminine. In place of masculine self-assertion, Keats seemingly adopts a disarming, feminine passivity – a femininity which frequently troubled or irritated his contemporaries. As I mentioned in the last section, my discussion of Keats therefore explores the extent of Keats's femininity (or 'effeminacy') and, as it does so, broadens the scope of the book to consider another important, but until recently often neglected Romantic genre, that of the drama. My focus on a variety of different forms of the drama in the final three chapters is informed by the growing critical awareness of the performative nature of social constructions of masculinity and femininity which I discussed earlier. Particularly in Keats's *Otho the Great*, I look at the ways in which the genre of the drama helps to expose the 'performative' nature of gender as described by Judith Butler and, in analysing Keats's gendered theories of dramatic performance, I suggest ways in which his poetical 'effeminacy' belies a troubled masculinity. My reading corroborates Julie A. Carlson's observation that an understanding of the Romantic drama is 'indispensable to an analysis of gender relations in the romantic age'.[35]

Unlike Keats's *Otho the Great*, Lord Byron's *Manfred: A Dramatic Poem* was never intended for the stage. What Byron provides us with is an example of a further significant Romantic form – the closet drama: a poem which possesses most of the properties of a play but is intended to be read rather than performed. The closet drama implicitly operates within the context of binary oppositions, such as that between mind and body, which during this period resonate with the language of gender difference. The many ways in which Byron's unperformable play constantly evokes the performance it denies reveals much about the instabilities of contemporary masculine identity. Of all the canonical Romantic poets, Byron is the one who sits most awkwardly alongside his fellow writers. As a poet, his sensationalist oriental tales, his satirical impulse and his proclaimed affinity with Augustan poetics mark him out as somewhat different from the other members of the 'Big Six'.[36] My choice of *Manfred* as a focus of study is therefore partly due to the generic interest outlined above but also to the fact that, whilst it evidently depicts a version of the so-called 'Byronic Hero' to be found in such works as *Childe Harold's Pilgrimage* and *Don Juan*, *Manfred* is, in addition, an obviously 'Romantic' text in its serious exploration of a Promethean theme.

Like *Manfred*, Shelley's *Prometheus Unbound* (which develops the Promethean theme in a very different manner) is a closet drama but it is one that is far more self-consciously engaged with the gender implications of its complex generic strategies. In this way, if in no other, this makes *Prometheus Unbound* perhaps the most challenging (as well as perhaps the most difficult) poem discussed in the book as a whole. Shelley's poem provides a fitting conclusion to my study of gender and genre in the Romantic poets in that it not only deals directly with the gendered relationship between men and women and deploys poetic genre as a vehicle for such engagement, but also offers a vision of what could be achieved if the injustice and inequality associated with contemporary constructions of gender difference were to be eradicated.

## NOTES

1 Marilyn Butler, *Romantics, Rebels and Reactionaries: English Literature and Its Background 1760–1830*, p.8. For a more inclusive overview of recent developments in Romantic criticism than I am able to offer here, see the Introduction to Cynthia Chase (ed.), *Romanticism*.

2 See, for example, Anne K. Mellor's provocative juxtaposition of John Keats and Emily Bronte in *Romanticism and Gender*.

3 Jerome McGann, 'Rethinking Romanticism', pp.735–6.

4 M.H. Abrams, 'English Romanticism: The Spirit of the Age', reprinted in *The Correspondent Breeze*, p.46.

5 Abrams, 'English Romanticism', pp.46–7.

6 Arden Reed (ed.), *Romanticism and Language*, p.15.

7 Reed, *Romanticism and Language*, pp.17–18.

8 As perhaps an extreme example of this see Jacques Derrida's essay on Percy Shelley's 'Living On: Border Lines', in Harold Bloom et al., *Deconstruction and Criticism*.

9 Stephen Copley and John Whale (eds), *Beyond Romanticism: New Approaches to Texts and Contexts 1780–1832*, pp.3–4.

10 Jerome J. McGann, *The Romantic Ideology: A Critical Investigation*, pp.32–3. Historicist Romantic criticism has taken many forms, illustrated, for example, by the diverse approaches of Marilyn Butler, Marjorie Levinson and, even, the playfully post-structuralist Jerome Christensen (see, in particular, Christensen's impressive *Lord Byron's Strength: Romantic Writing and Commercial Society* (1993)). For an attempt to provide a synthesising overview of some of these approaches, see Marjorie Levinson's essay 'The New Historicism: Back to the Future' in Marjorie Levinson, Marilyn Butler, Jerome McGann and Paul Hamilton, *Rethinking Historicism: Critical Readings in Romantic History* (1989). For a more critical overview, see also Philip W. Martin's essay 'Romanticism, History, Historicisms', in Kelvin Everest (ed.), *Revolution in Writing* (1991). Steve Clark and David Worrall, themselves calling for renewed historicist criticism, take issue with what they perceive to be McGann's failure to construct a theoretically convincing methodology. For example, they write that 'the self-consciousness envisaged is, in its way, as recessive and disabling as the familiar deconstructive paradoxes. We are in history therefore our actions are culturally determined; our freedom lies in our proclamation of the impossibility of autonomous choice' (Steve Clark and David Worrall (eds), *Historicizing Blake* (1994), p.14).

11 McGann, *Romantic Ideology*, p.36.

12 McGann, *Romantic Ideology*, p.134.

13 Of the many books and essays which one could cite, the following represent some of the more obvious contributions: Margaret Homans, *Women Writers and Poetic Identity* (1980), Mary Poovey, *The Proper Lady and the Woman Writer* (1984), Anne K. Mellor (ed.), *Romanticism and Feminism* (1988), Stuart Curran, 'Romantic Poetry: The I Altered' in *Romanticism and Feminism*, Meena Alexander, *Women in Romanticism: Mary Wollstonecraft, Dorothy Wordsworth and Mary Shelley* (1989), Marlon B. Ross, *The Contours of Masculine Desire: Romanticism and the*

*Rise of Women's Poetry* (1989), Anne K. Mellor, *Romanticism and Gender* (1993).

14 Quoted in Sandra M. Gilbert and Susan Gubar, ' "But oh! that deep romantic chasm": The Engendering of Periodization', p.81.

15 Mellor, *Romanticism and Feminism*, p.8. One would want, of course, to add poetry written by women to the list of silenced 'narratives' that Mellor provides here.

16 Copley and Whale, *Beyond Romanticism*, p.10.

17 Susan J. Wolfson, Review of Gene W. Ruoff (ed.), *The Romantics and Us: Essays on Literature and Culture* (1990) and Kenneth R. Johnston et al. (eds), *Romantic Revolutions: Criticism and Theory* (1990), *Studies in Romanticism*, 32 (spring 1993), p.130.

18 Pierre Macherey, *A Theory of Literary Production* (1986), quoted in McGann, *Romantic Ideology*, p.155.

19 Irene Taylor and Gina Luria, 'Gender and Genre: Women in British Romanticism', in Marlene Springer (ed.), *What Manner of Woman* (1977), p.120.

20 Anne Mellor, although she appears to argue against this simple gendering of genre, appears, in practice, to support it. Jacqueline Labbe, in a review of Mellor's *Romanticism and Gender*, notes pointedly that 'despite her own astute argument *against* gendering genres in the Introduction, the body of her text reinscribes the notion that the novel is a primarily feminine genre, since so many of her ideas are derived from novels. ... By almost totally defining feminine Romanticism through novels and the odd tract, Mellor *conforms* to, instead of disputing, a standard gendering of genre' (Jacqueline M. Labbe, Review in *The Wordsworth Circle*, 25.4 (autumn 1994), p. 262. In addition to this, I have doubts about the usefulness of the terms 'masculine' and 'feminine' Romanticism when one is applied almost exclusively to male writers and the other to female writers: as Labbe suggests, Mellor argues against such deterministic reading in her Introduction but seems to support it through the examples she provides in the remainder of the book.

21 Stuart Curran, 'Women Readers, Women Writers', in Stuart Curran (ed.), *The Cambridge Companion to British Romanticism* (1993), p.193.

22 Mellor, *Romanticism and Gender*, p.4. For my reservations about Mellor's undoubtedly useful and timely book, see note 20 above.

23 'La Loi de genre' was first published in *Glyph* 7 (1980) with an English translation by Avital Ronell. The text used here is a slightly modified version of that translation taken from Jacques Derrida, *Acts of Literature*, ed. Derek Attridge (1992), p. 224.

24 See Stuart Curran, *Poetic Form and British Romanticism* (1986). For another view on Romanticism and genre, see Clifford Siskin, *The Historicity of Romantic Discourse* (1988) – which I discuss in Chapter 2.

25 Derrida, 'The Law of Genre', pp. 230–1.

26 Derrida, 'The Law of Genre', p. 227.

27 Derrida, 'The Law of Genre', p.243.

28 For the purposes of the present book, I have chosen to read Cixous's writings as deconstructive in their tendencies and thus offering an incisive critique of how gender relations are brought into play within west-

ern society. Having said this, I am also aware of the many criticisms of her work which accuse it, amongst other things, of ultimately espousing a fundamentally essentialist position in its championing of the notion of an *écriture féminine*. Toril Moi, for example, records not only the presence of 'biologism' in her theories but also a decidedly anti-Derridean proclivity: 'Fundamentally contradictory, Cixous's theory of writing and femininity shifts back and forth from a Derridean emphasis on textuality as difference to a full-blown metaphysical account of writing as voice, presence and origin' (*Sexual/Textual Politics: Feminist Literary Theory*, p.119).

29  'Sorties' was originally published in *La Jeune Née* (1975). The sections directly used in this chapter were translated into English by Ann Liddle and published firstly in New French Feminisms (ed. Marks and de Courtivron, 1980). The present text of this translation is taken from David Lodge (ed.), *Modern Criticism and Theory: A Reader*, (1988). Passage quoted from pp.287–8.

30  G.J. Barker-Benfield, *The Culture of Sensibility*, p.104.

31  For a historical context for this, see J.G.A. Pocock, *Virtue, Commerce, and History*, p.114: 'Economic man as masculine conquering hero is a fantasy of nineteenth-century industrialisation ... His eighteenth-century predecessor was seen as on the whole a feminised, even an effeminate being, still wrestling with his own passions and hysteria and with interior and exterior forces let loose by his fantasies and appetites, and symbolised by such archetypically female goddesses of disorder as Fortune, Luxury, and most recently Credit herself.'

32  Judith Still and Michael Worton, *Textuality and Sexuality*, p.45. Michael McKeon has attempted to trace the origins of gender difference during the eighteenth century and has suggested that the 'effeminate' man enters cultural discourse as a third term which is distinguishable from both the masculine and the feminine and which is increasingly identified with the sodomite. Yet he also notes that 'the apprehension of "effeminacy" in eighteenth-century England was a very general mode of social analysis that articulated a wide range of convictions, from the traditional ideology of civic humanism to the innovative ideology of sensibility' (see McKeon, 'Historicizing Patriarchy: The Emergence of Gender Difference in England 1660–1760', especially p.308 and p.320 n.56). My own understanding of the term would suggest that even if 'effeminacy' achieves a distinctive identity within the period it is still none the less an identity which is read by contemporaries in relation to notions of masculinity and femininity. For a detailed survey of eighteenth-century notions of effeminacy, particularly in relation to the rise of 'sensibility' and commerce in eighteenth-century culture, see G.J. Barker-Benfield, *The Culture of Sensibility*, especially Chapter 3. For further discussion of sensibility in general – with more direct reference to its relationship with Romanticism – see Chris Jones, 'Radical Sensibility in the 1790s' and Chris Jones, *Radical Sensibility: Literature and Ideas in the 1790s*.

33  Judith Butler, 'Performative Acts and Gender Constitution: An Essay in Phenomenology and Feminist Theory', in *Performing Feminisms*, ed. Case, p. 271. For a fuller exposition of Butler's theories, see her book

*Gender Trouble*.

34 See Mary Jacobus, *Romanticism, Writing, and Sexual Difference*.

35 Julie A. Carlson, *In the Theatre of Romanticism*, p.19.

36 See, for example, McGann, *The Romantic Ideology*, pp. 24–7 for a discussion of Byron's effective exclusion from definitions of the 'Romantic'. The present book, on the other hand, excludes the work of William Blake which has often been a central feature of attempts to define Romanticism. The reasons for this exclusion stem mainly from my belief that to begin to understand fully Blake's generic strategies one has to engage in detail with a wide range of traditionally non-literary discourses. For an examination of some of these extra-literary discourses, see, for example, Jon Mee, *Dangerous Enthusiasm*; for attempts to relate Blake's work to more traditional generic categories, see, for example, Stuart Curran, *Poetic Form and British Romanticism* and Philip Cox, '"Among the Flocks of Tharmas": *The Four Zoas* and the Pastoral of Commerce'.

# 1

# Samuel Taylor Coleridge and Anna Laetitia Barbauld

## Gender, genre and pastoral

### I

My aim in this first chapter is to explore various permutations of the binary opposition between 'masculine' and 'feminine' as it appears in two poems from the 1790s (one poem by Samuel Taylor Coleridge and the other by Anna Laetitia Barbauld) and, in pursuing this binary as a fundamental structuring principle within the pastoral vision offered by both poets, I shall be using those interpretative strategies derived from the theoretical work of Jacques Derrida and Hélène Cixous which were discussed in the Introduction. However, it is important to register at the outset that such binary oppositions are never simple and, furthermore, that they are never divorced from the social and cultural contexts in which they operate. In her essay 'Pandora's Box: Subjectivity, Class and Sexuality in Socialist Feminist Criticism', Cora Kaplan makes the crucial observation that 'Masculinity and femininity do not appear in cultural discourse, any more than they do in mental life, as pure binary forms at play. They are always, already, ordered and broken up through other social and cultural terms, other categories of difference.'[1] My concern, then, is to demonstrate how the binary oppositions of masculine and feminine are mediated through the 'other categories of difference' to be found within the 'cultural discourse' of literary pastoral and to demonstrate how the ambiguities of the cultural constructions of gender in the 1790s are displaced on to the language of poetic genre. To write, or to write about, pastoral is also to write, or write about, the perceived inequalities of gender difference. Yet, as Kaplan would also argue, to write about gender difference is also to write about other social, political and economic differences which are always, already, at play within any cultural discourse. Whilst my initial concern might appear narrowly literary, therefore, the ultimate aim is to gesture towards an understanding of the larger role of the male and female poet during the unsettling final decade of the eighteenth century.

Pastoral is a particularly apposite genre with which to initiate an enquiry along these lines in that it depends upon a fundamental opposition – that between the country and the city – which frequently utilises images of masculine encroachment upon a feminine passivity. The masculine public world is played off against the private, feminised space of rural retirement and, whilst each gains its distinctive identity in opposition to the other, they also exist in what is ultimately a symbiotic relationship: the significance of the rural landscape cannot be appreciated without an awareness of the urban environment with which it is implicitly or explicitly contrasted. In addition to this fundamental dynamic of the genre, Romantic poetry further complicates the binary structures of pastoral by its introduction of the sublime experience into the 'beautiful' scenery of the countryside. In *A Philosophical Enquiry into the Origin of our Ideas of the Sublime and Beautiful*, first published in 1757, Edmund Burke had clearly differentiated the two terms of his enquiry along gendered lines. Thus when he comes to offer a direct comparison between the Sublime and the Beautiful, the distinctions he makes resonate with the unspoken assumptions of gender difference:

For sublime objects are vast in their dimensions, beautiful ones comparatively small; beauty should be smooth, and polished; the great, rugged and negligent; beauty should shun the right line, yet deviate from it insensibly; the great in many cases loves the right line, and when it deviates, it often makes a strong deviation; beauty should not be obscure; the great ought to be dark and gloomy; beauty should be light and delicate; the great ought to be solid, and even massive.[2]

As David Simpson observes, '[m]ilitant masculinity in control of absolute power is thus the natural possessor of sublimity. Pleasure, love, and harmony, the attributes of the beautiful, are reciprocally feminised.'[3] In the feminised beauty of a pastoral landscape, therefore, the masculinised sublime might be seen as an attempt to regain a masculine control and authority. However, these oppositions (and oppositions within oppositions) are often far from stable. Whilst there is a desire, as I will demonstrate, to order the sublime and beautiful elements within the landscape – or 'hierarchize' them (to use Cixous's term) – and usually to give some kind of priority to the 'masculine' element, the wider generic instability discussed by Derrida in his essay on genre means that such Romantic, masculine self-assertion is always deeply troubled. Simpson observes that the 'very reliance of the language of the sublime upon the tropes of excess always threatened the collapse of its [Burke's] claim to authority into a merely feminised disorder'.[4] It is this constant threat of disruption which provides the underlying dynamics of Coleridge's poem.

The poem now known as 'Reflections on having left a Place of Retirement' had a significantly different title when Coleridge first published it in the *Monthly Magazine* in 1796 under the heading 'Reflections on entering into active life'. This difference would seem to suggest a fundamental uncertainty as to the focus of the poem: is its chief concern that of depicting the benefits to be gained from 'Retirement' (thus marking the poem as pastoral in an important sense) or is it primarily aiming to display the exigencies and moral demands of an 'active life' (a life which, by implication, rejects the lures of a pastoral haven)? This tension is, of course, at the heart of the poem, but the fact that such potential confusion continues into two opposing title alternatives suggests that the tension is one that, at an important level, remains unresolved. Furthermore, in his different titles, Coleridge also indicates doubts about the relationship between his text and the discourse of poetry. The full title of the first version reads: 'Reflections on entering into active life. A Poem which affects not to be poetry'. To the later title he added a Latin tag from Horace: 'Sermoni propriora' – which he jokingly translated in a letter as 'Properer for a Sermon'.[5] Both of these sub-headings exhibit an uncertainty about the nature of the poem's discourse, an uncertainty which can be related to a tension between the public and the private. On the one hand, Coleridge fears that his poem degenerates into oratory and thus ceases to be poetry; on the other hand there seems to be the implication that the discourse of the public speaker is that which is required to support an 'active life' as opposed to the 'retired' voice of the pastoral poet. This indecision needs of course to be read in the context of the fact that the public/private binary opposition is a major structuring antithesis for pastoral as a genre. Drawing upon the ideas of Derrida discussed earlier in the chapter, we can see that by 'marking' his text in one way, through a specific choice of title, Coleridge is also 'de-marking' it and creating an awareness of the poem's other focus which the alternative title more explicitly gestures toward. It is, then, a poem of pastoral 'retirement' but also a poem about 'active life'; it functions as the 'personal' discourse of poetry but also associates itself with a more explicitly 'public' discourse which Coleridge implies is analogous to that of the sermon.

These doubts and uncertainties about genre and discourse more generally can be related to issues of gender difference. This is evident as the poem unfolds:

> Low was our pretty Cot: our tallest Rose
> Peep'd at the chamber-window. We could hear
> At silent noon, and eve, and early morn,
> The sea's faint murmur. In the open air
> Our Myrtles blossom'd; and across the porch
> Thick Jasmins twined: the little landscape round
> Was green and woody, and refresh'd the eye.
> It was a spot you might aptly call
> The Valley of Seclusion! Once I saw
> (Hallowing his Sabbath-day by quietness)
> A wealthy son of Commerce saunter by,
> Bristowa's citizen: methought, it calm'd
> His thirst for idle gold, and made him muse
> With wiser feelings: for he paus'd, and look'd
> With a pleas'd sadness, and gaz'd all around,
> Then eyed our Cottage, and gaz'd round again,
> And sigh'd, and said, it was a Blessed Place.
> And we *were* bless'd. (1–18)[6]

The 'Valley of Seclusion' is viewed as essentially feminine: a place of passivity and retirement and one that has its values delineated through the emblematic use of flowers (the rose is a traditional emblem of amorous love and, specifically, the amorous female; the jasmine and the myrtle are described by Coleridge in 'The Eolian Harp' as 'Meet emblems ... of Innocence and Love' (5)). Coleridge presents a harmonious view of early matrimony – the union of opposite genders – but his description omits one side of the equation. In this first section of the poem it is only with the arrival of the 'wealthy son of Commerce' that the 'masculine' is explicitly introduced. This businessman from Bristol is a representative of the 'public' world that lies outside the 'Valley of Seclusion' and his moral values appear to be diametrically opposed to the quasi-prelapsarian bliss of the newly wed lovers. Indeed, Coleridge is here presenting the businessman as a modern-day version of Satan from Milton's *Paradise Lost*. One recalls, for example, the entry of Satan into Eden in which Milton also makes use of the retirement trope:

Much he the place admired, the person more.
As one who long in populous city pent,
Where houses thick and sewers annoy the air,
Forth issuing on a summer's morn to breathe
Among the pleasant villages and farms
Adjoined, from each thing met conceives delight,
The smell of grain, or tedded grass, or kine,
Or dairy, each rural sight, each rural sound;
If chance with nymph-like step fair virgin pass,
What pleasing seemed, for her now pleases more,
She most, and in her look sums all delight. (9.444–54)[7]

Coleridge's text attempts to defuse the threat presented by this encroaching masculine force. The businessman seems to be transformed by the valley's peace and become almost 'blessed' in recognising its blessedness. However, one should remember that in *Paradise Lost* Satan too seems to be overcome for a moment but is not ultimately dissuaded from his nefarious intentions. In the present poem the businessman is unsettling because, even if he does represent an immoral thirst for 'idle gold', he also acts as an embodiment of the 'active life' which, as we have seen, is binarily opposed to the attainment of 'retirement'. This masculine encroacher upon the feminine 'Valley of Seclusion' is, then, also, ironically, a partial embodiment of the male poetic voice within the poem.

The innate tension introduced through the 'wealthy son of Commerce' surfaces again in the next section with its presentation of a Sublime moment:

                                    But the time, when first
From that low Dell, steep up the stony Mount
I climb'd with perilous toil and reach'd the top,
Oh! what a goodly scene! *Here* the bleak mount,
The bare bleak mountain speckled thin with sheep;
Grey clouds, that shadowing spot the sunny fields;
And river, now with bushy rocks o'er brow'd,
Now winding bright and full, with naked banks;
And seats, and lawns, the Abbey and the wood,
And cots, and hamlets, and faint city-spire;
The Channel *there*, the Islands and white sails,
Dim coasts, and cloud-like hills, and shoreless Ocean –
It seem'd like Omnipresence! God, methought,
Had built him there a Temple: the whole World
Seem'd *imag'd* in its vast circumference:

No *wish* profan'd my overwhelmed heart.
Blest hour! It was a luxury, – to be! (26–42)

I noted earlier how the Romantic sublime problematises the binary oppositions of Romantic pastoral in that, if pastoral relies upon what can simply be described as masculine city versus feminine country, then the sublime re-establishes a gendered opposition within a 'natural', pastoral setting. The masculine sublime is, at its most basic level, opposed to the feminine beautiful, and this is clearly in evidence in the present passage where the masculine poetic voice attempts to reassert itself in a form which is more acceptable than that represented by the businessman. The 'low' cot and dell are left behind as the speaker climbs the 'stony Mount' from where the entire pastoral landscape is seen to spread itself out subserviently to his gaze. The implicitly phallic mountain is opposed to the feminine river which is 'bright and full, with naked banks'. The opening description of pastoral bliss had attempted to exclude gender oppositions – here they are reasserted with a vengeance as masculine self-assertion takes over in an attempt to deny – or, at least, appropriate – the existence of a feminine other. As Anne Mellor observes about another of his poems, 'Coleridge annihilates the very difference that divides the self from the other, the human from the divine, and, implicitly, the male from the female'.[8] Coleridge's male gaze fixes and controls the feminised 'beautiful' landscape that lies beneath him and thus enables him to share God's apparent omnipotence and bring everything within the bounds of the 'vast circumference' of his own imaginative (self-)perception.

None the less, this section does not remain untroubled. Problems re-emerge with the introduction of the concept of luxury: 'Blest hour! It was a luxury, – to be!' This is a difficult line and one which sends many contradictory resonances through the poem. At face value it suggests the benevolence of God acting through nature. However, there is also the implicit suggestion that perhaps the excess suggested by 'luxury' would be more at home in the city as criticised from the frugal virtuousness of retirement. Again, then, the masculine speaker would seem to be aligning himself with the 'son of Commerce', imposing himself upon nature and converting it into something for his own use. What could be seen as God's beneficence could also be seen as Man's culpable excess.

David Aers, Jonathan Cook and David Punter note interestingly how there are certain implicit ideological affinities between Coleridge the poet and the Bristol businessman. In his portrayal of the businessman, Coleridge 'is actually representing what was already a characteristic attitude among the "wealthy" urban bourgeoisie to the country as an asocial and temporary retreat from the world of "Commerce", an attitude which he also, to some degree, shared'.[9] The fact that the poet's apparently ambiguous attitude is registered through the use of the word 'luxury' is in many ways to be expected in that the word itself was an ideologically overdetermined site within the cultural discourse of the eighteenth century. The complexity of semantic nuance encoded within the word is admirably charted by John Sekora in his book on the subject.[10] Broadly speaking, one can distinguish between two extreme positions in relation to the concept of luxury. The first is defined (though not subscribed to) by Bernard Mandeville in *The Fable of the Bees*:

It is a receiv'd Notion, that luxury is as destructive to the wealth of the whole Body Politic, as it is to that of every individual Person who is guilty of it ... What is laid to the Charge of Luxury besides, is, that it increases Avarice and Rapine: And where they are reigning Vices, offices of the greatest Trust are bought and sold; the Minister that should serve the Public, both great and small, corrupted, and the Countries every Moment in danger of being betray'd to the highest Bidder And lastly, that it effeminates and enervates the People, by which the Nations become an easy Prey to the first Invaders.[11]

The opposing view can be seen in Richard Payne Knight's *The Progress of Civil Society: A Didactic Poem in Six Books* which was published in 1796, the same year as the first version of Coleridge's poem, and which Sekora describes as offering 'a redaction into verse of the lessons of the *Wealth of Nations*':

> Each found the produce of his toil exceed
> His own demands, of luxury or need;
> Whence each the superfluity resign'd,
> More useful objects in return to find:
> Each freely gave what each too much possess'd
> In equal plenty to enjoy the rest.
>
> Hence the soft intercourse of Commerce ran,
> From state to state, and spread from clan to clan;
> Each link of social union tighter drew,
> And rose in vigour as it wider grew.[12]

Luxury, then, could be seen as socially divisive or socially cohesive; the destroyer of national prosperity or the basis for mercantile wealth. In terms of gender, luxury could lead to the masculine 'vigour' of Payne Knight's vision or it could be depicted as a force that 'effeminates and enervates the People'. Both Sekora and Tom Furniss, in a more recent essay on Edmund Burke, note that luxury in its pejorative sense in the eighteenth century and before is frequently gendered as feminine. Furniss relates this to his discussion of the Burkean Sublime and Beautiful and observes that 'Burke's representation of beauty draws on contemporary figurations of luxury and of the feminine as at once irresistibly alluring and physically and politically dangerous'.[13] For Furniss, Burke's sublime is 'a 'masculine' antidote to the beautiful'.[14] This may well be the case but it does little to resolve the problem presented by Coleridge's poem. What we are offered here is a version of the sublime, and not the beautiful, which is associated with the ambiguous attractions of 'luxury'. Indeed, I have suggested that the sublime experience upon the 'stony Mount' is in many ways configured as a more acceptable masculine alternative to the feminised (and beautiful) pastoral landscape of the poem's opening lines. How, then, can this be explained in terms of the structuring oppositions of masculine and feminine and also in terms of the underlying discourse of economic transaction which we have begun to uncover?

To approach an answer to this problem, we need to call again upon the work of Hélène Cixous. In 'Sorties' she writes that 'The specific difference that has determined the movement of history as a movement of property is articulated between two economies that define themselves in relation to the problematics of giving.'[15] These two 'economies' are related, inevitably, to the relationship between the masculine and the feminine. The masculine 'gift' is always dependent upon a return of some kind, it is a form of commercial transaction. The 'feminine' gift, on the other hand, is given freely, with no thought of self-advancement. What is crucial for the present passage is that the gendered attitude to 'giving' also has an effect on the ability to 'receive'. Cixous observes in 'Castration or Decapitation' that 'the moment you receive something you are effectively "open" to the other, and if you are a man you have only one wish, and that is hastily to return the gift, to break the circuit of an exchange that could have no end ... to be nobody's child, to owe no one a thing.'[16] If we return to Coleridge's poem we could describe the benevolence of the natural world as perceived from the 'stony Mount' as analogous to the generosity of the feminine 'gift'. At the moment of apparent masculine self-assertion through the sublime, therefore, the speaker is confronted with the threatening re-emergence of the feminine that, according to Cixous, acts as a challenge to his masculinity which is unable to accept such a 'gift'. Masculine commercial activity (registered within the poem by the presence of the businessman) is critically divided in its attitude towards 'luxury': on the one hand it rejects it as a feminine lure towards inactivity and debilitating lethargy; on the other it recognises that a surplus is the necessary prerequisite for all commercial transaction. Coleridge's poet persona is caught within the same (masculine) dilemma: in order to produce his poetry, the bourgeois poet requires the luxuriant excess of the natural world. However, the reverse is not true: the natural world does not require the productions of the poet in order to validate its existence. The poet and the merchant both try to control and exploit surplus (luxury) but at the same time live in fear of being controlled and exploited by the same force. The language of commerce finds expression in the language of poetry and both are mediated through the dialectics of gender difference.

In her discussion of male Romantic poetry in *Women Writers and Poetic Identity*, Margaret Homans notes that 'When Mother Nature and other feminine figures are objectified as the other, they may be possessed or become the property of the subject'.[17] She proceeds to note that 'appropriation is the relationship between the self-centred Romantic speaker or poet and the feminine objects about which he writes'. In the present poem, however, this 'appropriation' (linked as it is to the ideology of commercial exploitation) is radically challenged by a subversive return of the feminine 'object' as active agent. Jane Moore makes some observations about the Romantic sublime which can usefully be read as a gloss upon the dynamics of Coleridge's poem. She writes that:

Not only does woman introduce the lack which makes sublimity both desirable and impossible, she also, like the sublime, seduces and tyrannizes the poet. As always other than the subject, always outside the subject's reach, ineffable and inexpressible, the sublime object exposes the lack which is the cause and symptom of his desire; so too does the figure of woman.[18]

Attempting to assert his masculinity within the feminised retirement landscape, Coleridge confronts the sublime as he climbs the 'mount' only to be confronted in turn by the very femininity he was attempting to overcome. The presence of the feminised 'luxury' within the sublime is thus the occasion for the poet both to reject and be rejected by the landscape of retirement. The speaker concludes:

> Ah! quiet Dell! dear Cot, and Mount sublime!
> I was constrain'd to quit you. Was it right,
> While my unnumber'd brethren toil'd and bled,
> That I should dream away the entrusted hours
> On rose-leaf beds, pampering the coward heart
> With feelings all too delicate for use?
> Sweet is the tear that from some Howard's eye
> Drops on the cheek of one he lifts from earth:
> And he that works me good with unmov'd face,
> My benefactor, not my brother man!
> Yet even this, this cold beneficence
> Praise, praise it, O my Soul! oft as thou scann'st
> The sluggard Pity's vision-weaving tribe!
> Who sigh for Wretchedness, yet shun the Wretched,
> Nursing in some delicious solitude
> Their slothful loves and dainty sympathies!
> I therefore go, and join head, heart, and hand,
> Active and firm, to fight the bloodless fight
> Of Science, Freedom, and the Truth in Christ.
>
> Yet oft when after honourable toil
> Rests the tir'd mind, and waking loves to dream,
> My spirit shall revisit thee, dear Cot!
> Thy Jasmin and thy window-peeping Rose,
> And Myrtles fearless of the mild sea-air.
> And I shall sigh fond wishes – sweet Abode!
> Ah! – had none greater! And that all had such!
> It might be so – but the time is not yet.
> Speed it, O Father! Let thy Kingdom come! (43–end)

The masculine speaker has to reject not only the obviously feminine cot and dell but also the more problematic sublime experience offered by the 'Mount sublime'. There is a clear rejection of feminine pamperings, feelings and delicacies in favour of a more overtly masculine activity within society rather than the feminine domain of pastoral retirement. The feminine is never far away, though, making its return through the poet's reference to the tears of John Howard (1726–90), the prison reformer and philanthropist:

> Sweet is the tear that from some Howard's eye
> Drops on the cheek of one he lifts from earth.

Although one might see this as a more controlled appropriation of feminine qualities by masculine discourse, it does none the less repeat the underlying pattern of the poem as a whole. Throughout there is a constant oscillation between the two poles of the masculine and the feminine with no hope of a harmonious reconciliation between the two. The assertion of the masculine continually brings about the resurgence of its opposite. The only hope offered at the end of the poem is an appeal to a transcendent Christianity and a spiritual future. Here too, however, the vision is inevitably compromised for the same reasons. At first this redeeming future appears to be embodied in a version of the opening pastoral landscape of retirement, a landscape which we have identified as essentially feminine. Yet, as the poem moves towards its climax, this is replaced by a more traditional appeal to a heavenly 'Father' who is to establish his eternal 'Kingdom' – a kingdom centred, as we know from Revelation, on the holy city of Jerusalem.

Coleridge's poem commences as a celebration of harmony and reconciliation between the sexes. Its unfolding reveals the structures of discourse that render such a vision impossible. In a struggle to produce meaning the possibility of reconciliation recedes and the poem ends with an appeal not to life but to death. To quote Cixous once more: 'the movement by which each opposition is set up to produce meaning is the movement by which the couple is destroyed. A universal battlefield. Each time a war breaks out. Death is always at work.'[19]

## II

Anna Barbauld's poem 'To Mr. C – – – GE' was first published in the *Monthly Magazine* in 1799.[20] The poem dates from 1797 and, as Roger Lonsdale notes, 'was no doubt written after a visit by the 24-year-old Coleridge to Mrs. Barbauld in Bristol' in August of that year.[21] In many ways the poem appears as a repetition of Coleridge's own apparent self-admonition in 'Reflections'. In the earlier poem, the speaker effectively chastises himself for nearly succumbing to the temptations of luxurious retirement when there are more urgent needs to be confronted within the busy scenes of social life. This

rejection of the retirement motif is mirrored in Barbauld's poem
where the speaker warns the youthful Coleridge against the lures,
expressed in pastoral terms, of an abstracted 'metaphyical lore'. The
poem moves towards the conclusion that

> Active scenes
> Shall soon with healthful spirit brace thy mind:
> And fair exertion, for bright fame sustained,
> For friends, for country, chase each spleen-fed fog
> That blurs the wide creation. (38–42)

In urging Coleridge towards 'active scenes' the poem re-enacts the
rejection of a feminine pastoral inactivity in favour of vigorous masculine social endeavour.

Barbauld not only rehearses the general theme of Coleridge's
poem, then, but also replicates the fundamental structuring oppositions of the earlier text. In depicting her landscape of deceptive feminine pastoral, she implicitly conflates Coleridge's beautiful 'Valley of
Seclusion' with his sublime experience of the 'stony Mount'. The
result is a quasi-allegorical landscape of enchantment:

> MIDWAY the hill of science, after steep
> And rugged paths that tire unpractised feet,
> A *grove* extends; in tangled mazes wrought,
> And filled with strange enchantment: – dubious shapes
> Flit through dim glades, and lure the eager foot
> Of youthful ardour to eternal chase.
> Dreams hang on every leaf: unearthly forms
> Glide through the gloom; and mystic visions swim
> Before the cheated sense. Athwart the mists,
> Far into vacant space, huge shadows stretch
> And seem realities; while things of life,
> Obvious to sight and touch, all glowing round,
> Fade to the hew of shadows – *Scruples* here
> With filmy net, most like autumnal webs
> Of floating gossamer, arrest the foot
> Of generous enterprise; and palsy hope
> And fair ambition with the chilling touch
> Of sickly hesitation and bleak fear.
> Nor seldom *Indolence*, these lawns among,
> Fixes her turf-built seat; and wears the garb
> Of deep philosophy, and museful sits,
> In dreamy twilight of the vacant mind,
> Soothed by the whispering shade; for soothing soft
> The shades; and vistas lengthening into air,

With moon-beam rainbows tinted – there each mind
Of finer mould, acute and delicate,
In its high progress to eternal truth
Rests for a space, in fairy bowers entranced;
And loves the softened light and tender gloom;
And, pampered with most unsubstantial food,
Looks down indignant on the grosser world,
And matter's cumbrous shapings. (1–32)

In this landscape which looks back to Spenser and forward to Keats, Barbauld combines her version of the aloof masculine self-assertion of Coleridge's sublime experience which 'looks down indignant on the grosser world' with the deceptive enchantments of a pastoral retreat. In doing this, the poem essentially repeats the dual Coleridgean rejection of both 'Valley' and 'Mount'. For Barbauld, the pastoral landscape is only validated as a temporary 'rest' from more urgent public pursuits. Here she tacitly echoes the philosophy of the sauntering businessman from Bristol in Coleridge's poem and also of Coleridge himself in relation to pastoral poetry which, he implicitly claims, can only be written and enjoyed, like retirement itself, after the fulfilment of higher objectives.

At one level, therefore, Barbauld's poem could be seen as a fairly uncomplicated re-writing of the male poet's earlier text. It does, admittedly, replace a general sense of pastoral retirement with a more specific 'metaphysic lore' but, none the less, the general structuring principles remain very similar. However, in pursuing an analysis of the poem, it is worth keeping in mind an observation made by Cora Kaplan in an essay entitled 'Language and Gender'. Kaplan observes that:

To be a woman and a poet presents many women poets with such a profound split between their social, sexual identity (their 'human' identity) and their artistic practice that the split becomes the insistent subject, sometimes overt, often hidden or displaced, of much women's poetry.[22]

In addressing Coleridge in a poem, Barbauld is presenting herself in the double identity of 'poet' and 'woman', an identity which in the 1790s was inevitably fissured. Barbauld's own anxiety about this identity is revealed in her comment that she had 'stepped out of the bounds of female reserve in becoming an author.'[23] As a poet, Barbauld offers herself to Coleridge as a fellow pursuer of 'eternal truth'; as a woman, she is potentially the troubling 'other' that the poet has

to reject in order to attain that same truth. And, to return to the ideas
of Jacques Derrida rehearsed at the beginning of this chapter, when
the female poet 'marks' herself as 'poet' (a masculine demarcation in
the 1790s) she also 'unmarks' herself and paradoxically foregrounds
her position as 'woman'.

Within the poem, these concerns are indirectly revealed through
Barbauld's use of the words 'delicate' and 'pampered'. Coleridge had
written of how, in his pastoral retirement, he was 'pampering the
coward heart / With feelings all too delicate for use' (47–8). For
Coleridge, the over-indulgent luxury suggested by 'pampering' is
aligned with the effeminacy of inactive 'delicacy'. Barbauld, on the
other hand, differentiates between a positive delicacy and a similarly
negative pampering. For her, the mind of a truly 'finer mould' is one
which is also 'acute and delicate' although it is none the less one that
is susceptible to the attractions of a retirement where it is 'pampered
with unsubstantial food'. Barbauld's championing of the 'delicate'
mind is only, of course, indicated in passing: she, like Coleridge,
focuses more explicitly on the bracing activities of the socially
engaged intelligence. However, her attitude towards the concept of
delicacy is not without significance.

Coleridge's rejection of 'feelings all too delicate for use' is linked to
his doubts about the validity of his own poetic activity. His concern,
he argues, is, or should be, directed towards his 'unnumber'd
brethren' who toil and bleed – that is, those, as the pun suggests,
whose lives remain outside the domain of poetic 'numbers'. However, by the end of the poem, he has partially redeemed the possibility of a masculine 'feeling' through the image of action generated by
an empathising sensibility:

> Sweet is the tear that from some Howard's eye
> Drops on the cheek of one he lifts from earth. (50–1)

Here feeling is active in a way that it could not be for a woman. Cora
Kaplan, in 'Pandora's Box', notes how 'sensuality in men included a
strong positive element ... for the power of the imagination
depended upon it'. However, she proceeds to observe that 'No
woman of the same time could offer such an artistic manifesto. In
women the irrational, the sensible, even the imaginative are all
drenched in an overpowering and subordinating sexuality.'[24] By discovering a positive sensibility in the image of 'the tear from some
Howard's eye', Coleridge effectively redeems his poetic project: his

empathetic intelligence validates the productions of his imagination. In her support for the 'delicate' mind, Barbauld is attempting something similar, alerting her reader to the necessity for imaginative sensibility. However, she is advocating a virtue which, if put into practice by a woman, would be regarded as a vice. The positive 'delicacy' would either revert to the negative, feminised version that Coleridge initially rejects or would become the subversive transgression that Kaplan identifies.

Barbauld's poem tacitly attempts to negotiate this dilemma by implicitly introducing a more acceptable model of femininity into the text. Coleridge's poem had concluded with an apocalyptic appeal to the heavenly Father. Barbauld too ends with an appeal to heaven: 'Now heaven conduct thee with a parent's love!' However, the poem has anticipated the guiding care of a divine parent's 'love' and can thus be seen to be presenting the voice of the poet as ultimately adopting a 'parental' role. Barbauld in effect writes her speaker into a maternal subject position in relation to Coleridge the poet. In place of the 'unsubstantial food' with which the enchanting landscape threatens to pamper his delicate mind, Barbauld will provide the solid nourishment of maternal guidance. In adopting this quasi-maternal role, Barbauld forgoes her claim to equality with or equivalence to the poet whom she addresses. It will be remembered how Margaret Homans observed that 'When Mother Nature and other feminine figures are objectified as the other, they may then be possessed or become the property of the subject.'[25] In the present poem Barbauld effectively 'objectifies' herself in this way by adopting an acceptable stereotypical role in relation to Coleridge. Whilst apparently being in a position of authority – as the speaker who gives information and advice – Barbauld's persona ironically writes herself into a position of subservience. The poem directs its attentions to the requirements of a male poet and, in doing so, it implicitly invalidates the very space from which it originates. In presenting herself as a poet, Barbauld also paradoxically reveals that, as a woman, she is excluded from that very position. It is, in the words of Jacques Derrida quoted in the Introduction, 'a certain participation without belonging – a taking part in without being part of, without having membership of the set'.[26]

## NOTES

1 Cora Kaplan, 'Pandora's Box: Subjectivity, Class and Sexuality in Socialist Feminist Criticism', in *Sea Changes*, p. 149.

2 Edmund Burke, *A Philosophical Enquiry*, p.113.

3 David Simpson, *Romanticism, Nationalism, and the Revolt against Theory*, p.128. For a brief and accessible introduction to the gendered aspects of the Burkean and Kantian sublimes as they relate to the poetry of Wordsworth and Coleridge, see Anne Mellor, *Romanticism and Gender*, pp. 85–90.

4 Simpson, *Romanticism, Nationalism ...*, p.131.

5 For a fuller account of these issues see, for example, Norman Fruman, *Coleridge, the Damaged Archangel*, pp.299–300 and Kelvin Everest, *Coleridge's Secret Ministry*, pp.222–42. There are also interesting discussions of this poem to be found in David Aers, Jonathan Cook and David Punter, 'Coleridge: Individual, Community and Social Agency', in Aers, Cook and Punter (eds), *Romanticism and Ideology*, pp.82–102, and in Paul Magnuson, *Coleridge and Wordsworth*, pp.150–2.

6 The version of the poem quoted here is taken from *Poems*, ed. John Beer.

7 Milton, *Paradise Lost*, ed. Alastair Fowler. For further discussion of the relationship between Coleridge's poem and Milton's epic, see Schultz, 'Coleridge, Milton and Lost Paradise' and Gerard, 'Clevedon Revisited'.

8 Mellor, *Romanticism and Gender*, p.90. The poem being discussed is 'This Lime Tree Bower my Prison'.

9 *Romanticism and Ideology*, p.84.

10 Sekora, *Luxury: The Concept in Western Thought*.

11 Quoted in Sekora, *Luxury*, pp.66–7.

12 See Sekora. *Luxury*, p.107.

13 Tom Furniss, 'Gender in Revolution: Edmund Burke and Mary Wollstonecraft', p.69.

14 Furniss, 'Gender in Revolution', p.70.

15 Cixous, 'Sorties', p.289.

16 'La Sexe ou la tête' was first published in *Les Cahiers du GRIF* (1976); the English translation used here is by Annette Kuhn and published in *Signs*, 7.1 (1983). The quotation is to be found on p.48. For a discussion of Cixous's theory of 'gifts' see Toril Moi, *Sexual/Textual Politics*, pp.110–13; and Morag Shiach, *Hélène Cixous*, pp.21–2.

17 Margaret Homans, *Women Writers and Poetic Identity*, p.37.

18 Jane Moore, 'Plagiarism with a Difference; Subjectivity in "Kubla Khan" and *Letters written during a Short Residence in Norway and Denmark*', p.157.

19 'Sorties', pp.287–8.

20 *Monthly Magazine*, 7 (1799), pp.231–2. The text for the poem used here is taken from this source.

21 Roger Lonsdale (ed.), *Eighteenth-Century Women Poets*, p.530.

22 Kaplan, *Sea Changes*, p.71.

23 Quoted in Lonsdale (ed.), *Eighteenth-Century Women Poets*, p.300.

24 Kaplan, *Sea Changes*, p.158.

25 Homans, *Women Writers*, p.37.

26 Derrida, 'The Law of Genre', p.227.

# 2
# William Wordsworth
## Using genre to approach 'Tintern Abbey'

### I

Any discussion of Wordsworth's 'Tintern Abbey' in relation to issues of gender must begin by declaring its debt to the influential work of John Barrell in the final chapter of *Poetry, Language and Politics*. In describing what he calls the 'Uses of Dorothy', Barrell reveals how the poet's sister is aligned with a feminised 'language of the sense' (109)[1] as opposed to the more properly 'masculine' language of 'reflection' which is able to move away from immediate sensory experience and achieve the insights of abstract rational thought. Through this 'use' of the female presence within the poem, Wordsworth constructs a narrative whereby women will one day gain access to this apparently more advanced mode of thought (just as Dorothy will repeat her brother's moral and spiritual development) and thus the poem can be seen, in part, to rehearse such early feminist arguments as those put forward in Mary Wollstonecraft's *Vindication of the Rights of Woman* (1792). Having said this, however, Barrell also persuasively notes how such quasi-feminist elements are undermined by the fact that Dorothy's lesser status within the poem is crucial for the poet's sense of self-validation: she must remain at an earlier stage of development in order to ground William's own ontological progress. Whilst apparently advocating a change in the situation of women within society and society's recognition of their abilities, 'Tintern Abbey' finally, so the argument concludes, confirms their subservient position.

The present chapter will take Barrell's conclusions as one point of departure and attempt to extend his argument to a consideration of the relationship between gender and genre in Wordsworth's poem. In doing this it will also focus, like Barrell's chapter, on specific verbal and syntactic nuances within the text and their larger ideological significances. In approaching the poem in this way, it is useful to keep in mind certain observations that Barrell makes very early on in his study when he develops a reading of Wordsworth put forward by

Donald Davie in his book *Articulate Energy*. Barrell follows Davie in noting how key words within Wordsworth's work seem to avoid the assignment of definite 'meaning' and rely upon a creative or imaginative or sympathetic response on the part of the reader. These key words Barrell describes by the term 'fiduciary symbols' and proceeds to argue that

in Wordsworth's poetry, the meaning of such symbols depends not on any agreement as to the meaning of words prior to their utterance in any particular instance, but on the willingness to trust that they do have some meaning, that they are promissory notes which, one day, the banker will honour. This is a willingness that the poet will create in us by, and during, his utterance; and it is such a notion of symbols, of words whose meanings are not fixed, but whose relations with other words the poet attempts to suggest as he utters them, that will throw the weight of meaning in the poem on to its syntax.[2]

The consequences of such an argument can be seen to be far-reaching. The absence of a definitive 'meaning' which can be applied to words which appear to be central to an understanding of the poem could be interpreted as paving the way for the various nineteenth-century appropriations of the text that Richard Bourke highlights in his book *Romantic Discourse and Political Modernity*.[3] More generally, this reading foregrounds what one might term the productive uncertainty of 'Tintern Abbey', an uncertainty which is to be expected from a poem that depends upon a rhetorical strategy of visionary self-apotheosis juxtaposed with urgent self-questioning ('If this / Be but a vain belief' (50–1)). These shifts and modulations in the rhetorical register of the poem are largely what led Wordsworth to attempt a tentative generic categorisation in a note added to the 1800 edition of *Lyrical Ballads*: 'I have not ventured to call this Poem an Ode; but it was written with a hope that in the transitions, and in the impassioned music of the versification would be found the principal requisites of that species of composition.' In light of my discussion so far, it is the very tentative nature of this statement that makes it interesting: Wordsworth refrains from actually declaring his poem an ode, relying instead upon the response his utterance elicits from the reader who will have to 'find' and register certain qualities within the poem during the act of reading. Despite his 'hope' that the poem will be accepted as an ode, Wordsworth remains implicitly uncertain; as with the key words indicated by Barrell, the poem provides certain features which the reader has to relate one to the other in order to discover a generic 'meaning'.

In *Genres in Discourse* (1978; English translation, 1990), Tzvetan Todorov discusses the origin of genres and generic taxonomy and concludes that a search for origins is in many ways misguided: 'Where do genres come from? Quite simply from other genres ... There has never been a literature without genres; it is a system in constant transformation, and historically speaking the question of origins cannot be separated from the terrain of the genres themselves.'[4] What Todorov is implicitly offering here is a syntactical model of genres where the 'meaning' generated by a certain genre can at one level only be understood in relation to other genres both in the present and the past. Just as 'Tintern Abbey' relies upon its literal syntax for the communication of meaning, so, metaphorically, the significance of its generic claims can only be fully realised by paying due attention to the generic 'syntax' of literary history and contemporary literary practice. Synchronically, the poem intimates certain generic claims through a variety of rhetorical modulations; diachronically, it simultaneously positions itself within a range of generic histories. Both synchronically and diachronically it elicits from the reader an attempt to make it conform to certain generic categories. In his seminal study *Poetic Form and British Romanticism*, it is to this simultaneously synchronic and diachronic syntactical arrangement that Stuart Curran directs his critical focus:

The received traditions of literature, particularly as channeled through the centuries by their generic momentum, could compensate where other cultural embodiments had been emptied of palpable meaning. Against the failure of myth, the factionalism and proliferation of religious sects, the dissolution of iconographical knowledge, their resilient conceptual syntax kept its integrity and was thus able to counter and assimilate the demythologizing rationalism whose stream forged a new and dangerously rapid tributary in the eighteenth century.[5]

This is a rousing defence of the Romantic use of traditional generic forms and one where Curran reveals his own adherence to what Jerome McGann has famously entitled the 'Romantic Ideology'.[6] What is particularly significant for present purposes, though, is Curran's use of the term 'conceptual syntax' which suggests both that 'meaning' (or concepts) are communicated at a generic level and yet, at the same time, that this meaning can only be accessed through an awareness of how a specific poem is situated within a larger, syntactically arranged, generic system. Curran's description of the ways in which poems function generically implies (as is to be expected from his implicit espousal of the 'Romantic Ideology') the autonomy of the individual Romantic poet: the use of generic traditions is implicitly conveyed as a conscious act of resistance to unwelcome social and intellectual change in the present. Todorov, on the other hand, emphasises the representative role which genres assume within the society in which they are deployed: 'Like any other institution, genres bring to light the constitutive features of the society to which they belong.'[7] Genres might 'originate' and gain a certain kind of 'meaning' in relation to one another, but they also possess a significance which relates to the social conditions of their specific utterance. Curran's emphasis upon a poetic resistance to social change therefore needs to be modified in order to take into account the ways in which any generic usage is inevitably implicated in the social (or generic) systems ·that are apparently resisted and must, by its very nature, reveal what Todorov calls the 'constitutive features' of the ideology it appears to repudiate.

It was seen earlier that John Barrell reveals how certain key words in 'Tintern Abbey' possess 'meaning' only in relation to one another and that their role as 'fiduciary symbols' or 'promissory notes' places an increased emphasis upon the poem's syntax. The discussion of the work on genre by Tzvetan Todorov and Stuart Curran has shown how there is a similarity between this use of specific words in Wordsworth's poem and the ways in which genres function. Generic 'meaning' is not implicit but relational: genres have what Curran terms a 'conceptual syntax' , a syntax which, in use, brings to light what Todorov calls the 'constitutive features' of a specific society. The remainder of this chapter will explore the 'conceptual syntax' of 'Tintern Abbey' in light of the insights offered by Barrell, Todorov and Curran but will attempt to extend them through an application of the psychoanalytic methodology developed by Julia Kristeva in her essay 'Place Names' which, in its discussion of origins, childhood and language, seems highly pertinent to a study of the text currently under consideration.[8] Kristeva's observations enable the reader to explore in more detail the repressed nature of the poem's generic syntax, to pay further attention to the linguistic syntax of the text itself, and to relate both of these to the important issue of gender in the late eighteenth century. Before turning to the details of Kristeva's

chapter, however, it is necessary to explore in slightly more detail the
generic genealogy of 'Tintern Abbey'.

## II

In her important early study, *Tradition and Experiment in
Wordsworth's 'Lyrical Ballads' (1798)* (1976), Mary Jacobus notes that
'More than any other, "Tintern Abbey" is the poem for which
Wordsworth's predecessors had smoothed the way. But it is here,
where he is most uncritically indebted to the past, that his uniqueness is most strongly felt.'[9] In discussing the various ways in which
Wordsworth is 'indebted to the past' she spends considerable space
describing the importance of what she terms the 'revisit' poem and,
largely as a result of her analysis, it is now generally accepted that
poems such as Warton's 'To the River Lodon', Bowles's 'To the River
Itchen, near Winton' and Coleridge's 'To the River Otter' form part
of a generic tradition to which 'Tintern Abbey', with its return to the
Wye valley, can be related: poems which describe a quasi-elegiac
return to a place beloved in youth which provides the poetic persona
with the opportunity to lament usually painful changes that have
been inflicted by the passing of time. The opening of Wordsworth's
poem,

> Five years have passed; five summers, with the length
> Of five long winters! and again I hear
> These waters, rolling from their mountain-springs

thus immediately invites comparison with Coleridge's 'Sonnet. To
the River Otter':

> Dear native Brook! wild streamlet of the West!
>   How many various-fated years have passed,
>     What happy and what mournful hours, since last
> I skimm'd the smooth thin stone along thy breast

and, beyond that, with Thomas Warton's 'Sonnet. To the River
Lodon':

> Ah! what a weary race my feet have run,
> Since first I trod thy banks with alders crowned,
> And thought my way was all through fairy ground,
> Beneath thy azure sky, and golden sun.[10]

What has perhaps not been adequately commented upon is the fact that the majority of these 'revisit' poems are written as sonnets and that this establishes interesting generic tensions which generate significant meaning when read 'syntactically' in relation to Wordsworth's tentative claims for his poem's status as an ode. Whilst formally Wordsworth's poem is not a sonnet, its thematic concerns and its general tone suggest that the sonnet as genre is an important element of its generic genealogy and, indeed, it could even be suggested that Wordsworth's attempt to categorise the poem as an ode is a strategy designed to deny this genealogy. In attempting to approach 'Tintern Abbey' generically, therefore, it is important to establish at the outset the relationship between the ode and the sonnet and to delineate the gender inflections of a particular generic taxonomy.

Stuart Curran concludes his survey of the development of the ode by observing that 'By the time the history of the ode embarks on the century in which it was to become synonymous with lyric poetry, its greatest examples had already made conventional its nature as a dramatic, self-reflexive and dialectical form.'[11] Whilst one might see the sonnet as in some sense 'self-reflexive', in its evident foregrounding of its formal features, and 'dialectical' in its use of a turn or *volte*, it cannot be said to be 'dramatic' in the same way as an ode. The dramatic nature of the ode is impassioned but also invariably public in a way that is crucially different to the 'dramas' enacted in the smaller space of the sonnet. This difference is particularly evident if one looks at contemporary definitions of the sonnet genre. In his 'Introduction' to *A Sheet of Sonnets* (1796), for example, Coleridge offers the following account of what constitutes a true sonnet:

The sonnet, then, is a small poem, in which some lonely feeling is developed ... Poems, in which no lonely feeling is developed, are not sonnets because the Author has chosen to write them in fourteen lines; they should rather be entitled Odes, or Songs, or Inscriptions ... In a Sonnet then we require a development of some lonely feeling, by whatever cause it may have been excited; but those Sonnets appear to me to be most exquisite, in which moral Sentiments, Affections, or Feelings, are deduced from, and associated with, the scenery of Nature. Such compositions generate a habit of thought highly favourable to delicacy of character. They create a sweet and indissoluble union between the intellectual and the material world ... Hence the Sonnets of BOWLES derive their marked superiority over all other Sonnets; they domesticate with the heart, and become, as it were, a part of our identity.[12]

Unlike the more public voice of the ode, the sonnet is here described as focusing upon the 'lonely' poetic voice, the voice of the poet who is communing with the natural world. Whilst Coleridge emphasises the 'moral' function of the sonnet, he is also careful to speak in terms of 'Sentiments, Affections, or Feelings': this is a genre which aims to encourage a 'delicacy of character' and one which is removed from the strife of the public and social sphere. Significantly, Coleridge deploys the word 'domesticate' to describe the relationship between the sonnets of Bowles and their readership, a word which implicitly establishes the domain of the sonnet as feminised, a domestic, private and 'natural' environment opposed to the more 'masculine' world of public affairs and loftier literary genres. The sonnet was, after all, a genre which had in part been revived through the industry of female poets, particularly Charlotte Smith in her *Elegiac Sonnets* (first edition, 1784), as Coleridge acknowledges when he observes that 'Charlotte Smith and Bowles are they who first made the Sonnet popular among the present English: I am justified therefore by analogy in deducing its laws from *their* compositions.'[13] The sonnet was, then, a genre which could be seen as directly related to the productions of women poets and also implicitly feminised as regards its salient generic features.

In *Biographia Literaria* (1817), Coleridge returns to the influence of Bowles's poetry in terms which are again significant for their implicit alignment of gender and genre. He describes how as a young man he was prone to over-exertion of his intellectual powers until, like the devils in Milton's *Paradise Lost*, he 'found no end in wandering mazes lost'. He was rescued from this state, so he claims,

partly by an accidental introduction to an amiable family, chiefly, however, by the genial influence of a style of poetry, so tender, and yet so manly, so natural and real, and yet so dignified and harmonious, as the sonnets, &c of Mr. Bowles! Well were it for me perhaps, had I never relapsed into the same mental disease; if I had continued to pluck the flower and reap the harvest from the cultivated surface, instead of delving in the unwholesome quicksilver mines of metaphysic depths. But if in after time I have sought a refuge from bodily pain and mismanaged sensibility in abstruse researches, which exercised the strength and subtlety of the understanding without awakening the feelings of the heart; still there was a long and blessed interval, during which my natural faculties were allowed to expand, and my original tendencies to develope [*sic*] themselves: my fancy, and the love of nature, and the sense of beauty in forms and sounds.[14]

As in the earlier 'Introduction' to *A Sheet of Sonnets*, Coleridge estab-lishes a connection between the qualities and influences of the sonnet and those of a domestic environment: his movement to 'an amiable family' is akin in its effects to the reading of Bowles's sonnets. Coleridge ostensibly presents Bowles as a model of achieved balance between a series of binary oppositions, principally those relating to the mind/body or the human/natural divides. And, of course, as Hélène Cixous points out, all such binaries ultimately relate to the division between the social constructions of 'masculinity' and 'femi-ninity'.[15] Thus Bowles, according to the reading of him offered here, is 'tender' and yet 'manly', he has the ability to feel and yet also the ability to think: he is, as Coleridge observes slightly later, 'the first who reconciled the heart with the head'.[16] Having said this, it is also clear from the context of these pronouncements that Bowles is valued because he provides a counter-influence to the excessive 'mas-culine' intellectual activity that Coleridge felt himself to be threat-ened by. Bowles's sonnets, it could be argued, were welcomed because they delivered a necessary 'feminised' sensibility. It is further interesting to note that when he discusses the dangers of 'abstruse research', Coleridge initially quotes *Paradise Lost* concerning the devils' intellectual activity in hell and then introduces the metaphor of 'delving' in 'unwholesome quicksilver mines' which again takes the reader back to Milton's epic poem and the occupations of Satan and his legions. Given the status of Milton's Satan as a Romantic hero, one suspects Coleridge of glorying in his 'mental disease': there is something heroic, if necessarily fated, in this excessive 'masculine' activity. At a suppressed generic level, Milton's masculine (because intellectual) epic is being played off against Bowles's feminised son-neteering.

Evidence to support claims regarding the ambivalence of Cole-ridge towards the influence of Bowles's sonnets is provided by Coleridge himself. In a letter dated 10 September 1802 addressed to William Sotheby, Coleridge writes 'The truth is – Bowles has indeed the *sensibility* of a poet; but he has not the *Passion* of a great Poet. His latter Writings all want *native* Passion – Milton here & there supplies him with an appearance of it – but he has no native Passion, because he is not a Thinker.'[17] Although Coleridge is not necessarily writing of Bowles as a sonneteer here, this is a valid passage to bring to bear on the present argument because, for Coleridge, Bowles and certain aspects of the sonnet genre are almost invariably synonymous.

Coleridge in this letter notes that a certain 'passion' is a prerequisite for a 'great Poet' and yet this passion is not a 'feminine' excess but one associated with the poetry of Milton and the 'masculine' role of 'Thinker': Bowles is implicitly criticised for *failing* to achieve a satisfactory balance between the 'heart' and the 'head' and coming down too far on the side of the 'heart'. Even in *Biographia Literaria*, where Bowles is praised, other less able writers of sonnets are taken to task for their lack of mental application. Coleridge describes how he was moved to write and publish the three parodic 'Nehemiah Higgenbottom' sonnets which highlighted what he took to be the excesses of the 1790s fashion for sonneteering: 'Every reform, however necessary, will by weak minds be carried to an excess, that itself will need reforming.'[18] Coleridge implies that there is something potentially excessive – and perhaps threatening – in the sonnet genre as he has described it and, given that he is here writing of the politically turbulent decade of the 1790s, his use of the concept of 'reform' suggests that such threatening excess has a potentially significant political inflection.

Like Coleridge, Wordsworth as a young man came under the spell of Bowles's sonnets, a fact that he graphically described in later years in conversation with Samuel Rogers:

When Bowles's sonnets first appeared, a thin quarto pamphlet entitled *Fourteen Sonnets*, I bought them in a walk through London with my dear brother who was afterwards drowned at sea. I read them as we went along, and to the great annoyance of my brother, I stopped in a niche of London Bridge to finish the pamphlet.[19]

His interest and enthusiasm for sonnets and sonneteers continued throughout these early years: whilst he was an undergraduate he subscribed to the fifth edition of Smith's *Elegiac Sonnets* and, perhaps more importantly, he visited the poet in the November of 1791 just before his journey to France. On that occasion the meeting was not simply concerned with the understandable interest of a young poet in the work of a more established practitioner. In addition to possible poetic advice and encouragement, Smith also provided the young Wordsworth with letters of introduction to Helen Maria Williams and, probably, to one of the Deputies of the new Legislative Assembly.[20] The implicit metaphorical link established by Coleridge in *Biographia Literaria* between sonneteering and potentially excessive political radicalism is here given an interesting concrete basis. 'Tintern Abbey' is in many ways a poem about Wordsworth, writing at the end of the 1790s and after the tribulations caused by his confused responses to what he saw as the excesses of the French Revolution, attempting to come to terms with his own radical past. In tacitly evoking the 'revisit' sonnet tradition he also evokes his own past self of the 1790s and the dangerous excesses of a certain kind of sensibility. Like the sensibility associated with the sonnet inheritance, his earlier self within the poem is seen as 'feminised' and provided with a concrete feminine presence in the form of Dorothy whose youthful wildness, registered in her 'wild eyes' (120; 149) and 'wild ecstasies' (139), must be tempered by the poet's achieved 'masculine' maturity. In tentatively presenting the poem as an ode, Wordsworth indicates a desire to move towards a more socially responsible poetic voice.

### III

Wordsworth, as Curran observes, came to writing sonnets seriously very late in the day: it was not until the decade after the 1790s that he turned his attentions in a sustained fashion to this apparently lowly genre.[21] When he did start writing sonnets, it could be argued that he engaged upon a subtle critique of the 'revisit' tradition that he had inherited and which is seen to be a troubling presence in 'Tintern Abbey'. This revision of generic tradition is particularly evident in the poem ' "Beloved Vale!" I said, "when I shall con"':

> 'Beloved Vale!' I said, 'when I shall con
> Those many records of my childish years,
> Remembrance of myself and of my peers
> Will press me down: to think of what is gone
> Will be an awful thought, if life have one.'
> But, when into the Vale I came, no fears
> Distressed me; I looked round, I shed no tears;
> Deep thought, or awful vision, I had none.
> By thousand petty fancies I was crossed,
> To see the Trees, which I had thought so tall,
> Mere dwarfs; the Brooks so narrow, Fields so small.
> A Juggler's Balls old Time about him tossed;
> I looked, I stared, I smiled, I laughed; and all
> The weight of sadness was in wonder lost.

At one level this poem is a straightforward revision, and thus rejec-

tion, of the received 'revisit' conceit. The opening five lines of the
sonnet describe the by now traditional response to the revisited
scene, one where the poetic voice is moved to lament the passing of
time that the 'records' presented by the landscape bring to its attention. However, instead of describing this 'deep' or 'awful' mourning,
which would be a 'sadness' analogous to that associated with Bowles
or Smith, Wordsworth is keen to direct the reader to the sense of
'wonder' that a return to the natural world can elicit. The 'weight of
sadness' is removed by his return to the 'Vale' just as in 'Tintern
Abbey'

> the heavy and the weary weight
> Of all this unintelligible world
> Is lightened (40–3)

by the recollection of the 'forms of beauty' (24) offered by the Wye
valley. In this way Wordsworth's sonnet acts as a critique of the
'revisit' sonnet tradition and presents an apparently mature adult
vision which is able to laugh at the distance between himself as an
adult and his earlier childish self rather than finding in it a source of
melancholy. The laughter defies the 'elegiac' sonnets of Smith
together with those of her predecessors and contemporaries.

However, the presence of laughter is more problematic than this
suggests for, whilst the rejection of traditional poetic melancholy
would imply greater authorial autonomy and a mature independence, the laughter, together with the sense of authorial bewilder-
ment caused by the confusing discrepancies of scale between past and
present, would suggest that the poetic voice has become in an important sense child- rather than adult-like in its response. In his discovery of a wonderful delight in the juggling tricks of 'old Time', the
poet persona becomes like a child again despite the discrepancies
between child and adult vision that the sestet records. There seems
to be a radical ambiguity here, then, with the poet implicitly revealing both an achieved maturity and a regression to a pre-existing
immaturity. This is an ambiguity for which Julia Kristeva's essay
'Place Names' is able to provide a useful interpretative framework.

In 'Place Names', Kristeva is interested in exploring and defining
the 'infantile language' that exists during what she terms the 'semiotic *chora*', that time before entry into the 'symbolic' when the child
exists in a pre-symbolic, and yet none the less semiotic, relationship
with its mother's body. The child, embarked upon a process of self-

discovery, registers the spaces created within this relationship and responds to them with involuntary laughter:

During the period of indistinction between '*same*' and '*other*', infant and mother, as well as between 'subject' and 'object', while no space has yet been delineated (this will happen with and after the mirror stage – birth of the sign), the semiotic *chora* that arrests and absorbs the motility of the anaclitic facilitations relieves and produces laughter.[22]

The laughter of the child has an important function to perform, however, in that it acts in such a way as to record the experience that has produced it and thus anticipates the acquisition of language. The mother's body, the 'point of discharge' for the laughter it provokes, remains unfixed and confused until it is fixed in the child's awareness by the act of repetition which relies upon a sense of time being combined with a primary understanding of space:

Rhythm, a sequence of linked instants, is immanent to the *chora* prior to any signified spaciousness: henceforth, *chora* and rhythm, space and time coexist. Laughter is the evidence that the instance *took place*: the space that supports it signifies time. Located elsewhere, distant, permissive, always already past: such is the *chora* that the mother is called upon to produce with her child so that a semiotic disposition might exist.[23]

In Wordsworth's sonnet, the poet's return to mother nature as represented by the 'Beloved Vale' is effectively a return to the 'semiotic *chora*' as delineated by Kristeva. The poetic persona is confronted with a spatial confusion where size and distance refuse to be fixed and therefore knowable in relation to a sense of the 'self'. As in the 'semiotic *chora*', there is a collaboration between an awareness of 'space' and the presence of 'time' and, significantly in light of Kristeva's propositions, the movement of Time's 'Juggler's Balls' suggests 'rhythm' as well as confusion. The laughter produced by the speaker reproduces that of the child in that it functions in such a way as to overcome the confusion experienced and enable the poet to conclude the poem with an appearance of control: as an anticipation of symbolic language, the child's laughter registers a certain mastery over experience and a growing confidence in a sense of self in relation to the 'other'.

In writing a sonnet which apparently acts as a critique of the 'revisit' genre, Wordsworth seemingly asserts a masculine independence from a tradition which reveals a propensity towards a dangerously excessive feminine sensibility. None the less, in attempting such

a critique, Wordsworth risks a return to the equally 'feminised' space
of Kristeva's 'semiotic *chora*' which threatens the authority of the
(masculine) symbolic order with its re-opening of a primary uncertainty and indeterminacy. It is perhaps significant in light of this that
Wordsworth's most famous sonnets from this period refrain from
revisiting the 'revisit' genre and espouse instead the sonnet form
developed by Milton (and also explored by Coleridge in the 1790s).
In a letter from November of 1802, possibly written to Charles
Lamb, Wordsworth records his opinion that

Milton's Sonnets ... I think manly and dignified compositions, distin-
guished by simplicity and unity of object and aim, and undisfigured by
false or vicious ornaments. They are in several places incorrect, and
sometimes uncouth in language, and, perhaps, in some, inharmonious;
yet, upon the whole, I think the music exceedingly well suited to its end,
that is, it has an energetic and varied flow of sound crowding into
narrow room more of the combined effect of rhyme and blank verse than
can be done by any other kind of verse I know of.[24]

In place of the 'lonely' poetry of 'feminine' lament, Wordsworth con-
centrated upon the more overtly 'masculine' sonnets of public
address and social responsibility. Milton's sonneteering offered a
model that was 'manly' and 'energetic' and which was even prepared
to appear 'uncouth' in its desire to reject the feminine allurements of
unnecessary 'ornaments'.[25]

## IV

In *Tradition and Experiment*, Mary Jacobus suggested one potential
'usefulness' of Wordsworth's adoption of the 'revisit' poem as a
generic model for 'Tintern Abbey': 'The special usefulness of the
"revisit" poem lies with providing Wordsworth with a means of
asserting continuity as well as change – the continuity of the poet's
developing consciousness.'[26] The problem with a statement such as
this is that it fails to register the problematic nature of the notion of
'continuity' within 'consciousness'. In the analysis of the 'Beloved
Vale' sonnet it was seen how an attempt to deny disabling difference
between then and now produced within the poetic voice just such a
difference with the return of that voice to 'pre-symbolic' laughter
which anticipated adult language but was necessarily and significantly different from it. In 'Place Names', Kristeva discusses the role

played by the notion of the child in relation to rational adult discourse: a role which is 'unsettling' in that it presents the adult with an 'other' which is not simply a denial of human presence in the way that death is:

Reason was thus transcended by a *heterogeneous element* (biology: life) and by a *third party* (*I/you* communication is displaced by *it*: the child). These challenge the speaker with the fact that he is not whole, but they do so in a manner altogether different from that in which the obsessed person's wretched consciousness ceaselessly signifies his bondage to death. For, if death is the Other, life is a third party, and as this signification, asserted by the child, is disquieting, it might well unsettle the speaker's paranoid enclosure.[27]

The child, as an embodiment of 'life' as 'other', is initially a disturbing presence even though it performs a function which places it in opposition to that other 'other' within the adult's 'wretched consciousness': an awareness of 'death'. Kristeva proceeds to note how this unsettling child-presence is culturally transformed into a 'myth' which enables it to be appropriated into an adult discourse even when there is an apparent attempt to register childhood experience as somehow different to that of an adult. Her observations on this point are of particular relevance to 'Tintern Abbey' and, indeed, to Wordsworth's poetic project in its entirety (even though it is the work of Sigmund Freud that is specifically being discussed here):

Projected into the supposed place of childhood, and therefore universalized, one finds the features that are particular to adult discourse; the child is endowed with what is dictated by adult memory, always distorted to begin with; the myth of human continuity persists (from child to parent, sameness prevails).[28]

From Kristeva's viewpoint, the 'continuity of the poet's developing consciousness' that Jacobus traces via the generic genealogy of 'Tintern Abbey' is nothing more than a self-deluding 'myth'. Moreover, in attempting to 'revisit' the past, the poet is in danger of discovering an unsettling discontinuity rather than an enabling continuity, a discontinuity in which, according to Kristeva, the 'precocious, presymbolic organization is grasped by the adult only as a regression – jouissance or schizophrenic psychosis'.[29]

As has already been argued, Wordsworth's attempt to categorise his poem as an ode is part of a larger project which aims to disassociate it from the perceived dangers and excesses of the 'revisit' tradition, an attempt to proclaim a poetic 'masculine' maturity which speaks with an adult, public voice. Yet, just as in the 'Beloved Vale' sonnet, the dangers presented to this adult autonomy by the 'revisit' tradition can be seen to surface as a return of the repressed. It was seen how John Barrell alerts the reader to the necessity of paying renewed attention to the syntax of 'Tintern Abbey' in order to gain access to its meaning and such attention, in light of further comments made by Kristeva, can be as illuminating as analysis of the poem's generic syntax.

In her discussion of 'place names' (and it should be recalled that Wordsworth as a poet is particularly interested in poems on the naming of places), Kristeva notes that the 'primitive naming' of the child reveals certain verbal and syntactic traits:

Primitive naming very often makes use of adverbs of position, anaphoric demonstratives (*this, that*) or, more generally, 'topic' anaphora referring to an object either external or internal to the body proper and to the practical, immediate environment; observable in the first childhood verbalizations, it is always related to a space – a *point* that henceforth becomes *object* or *referent*.[30]

Kristeva proceeds to note that, whilst these tendencies might be a primary element within the linguistic activity of the child, they are none the less inevitably residually present within adult discourse and significantly reveal the genealogy of adult autonomy: 'These modalities, however, remain immanent to any usage of the demonstrative, as in all languages, since it is true ... that the archeology of *spatial naming* accompanies the development of the *subject unit*.'[31] In light of these observations, the opening section of 'Tintern Abbey' becomes particularly illuminating in terms of what its language reveals concerning its 'archeology'.

The opening paragraph of 'Tintern Abbey' famously describes the landscape of the Wye valley from the perspective of the poetic persona who surveys it. It is a description which at one level enacts a typical Romantic strategy of mapping an internal subjective vision on to an external 'reality':

> – Once again
> Do I behold these steep and lofty cliffs,
> Which on a wild secluded scene impress
> Thoughts of more deep seclusion. (4–7)

Where, the reader is led to ask, are these 'thoughts' meant to exist?

Wordsworth elides the external and the internal so that one reflects the other, giving a sense of communion with the natural world. However, this sense of communion could also be seen as dangerous for, in merging with what he beholds, the poet is in danger of losing his own sense of 'self'. Against this tendency of the poetic voice to lose its identity is a countering liguistic trait which can be related to Kristeva's observation of 'primitive naming'. The reference to the cliffs as 'these … cliffs' acts in such a way as to reinstate the observing self: against the movement towards communion with the land-scape is placed this linguistic marker of difference which establishes the presence of what Kristeva terms the 'subject unit' during the act of 'spatial naming'. Throughout the first section there is recourse to this linguistic strategy: 'These waters' (3), 'these … cliffs' (5), 'these plots of cottage ground' (11), 'These hedge-rows' (16), 'these pas-toral farms' (17) and (at the start of the next section) 'These forms of beauty' (24). This use of deixis reveals an insistent desire to mark out the poet as an autonomous observing presence who, whilst a 'worshipper of nature' (153), maintains a significant difference from both the 'coarser pleasures of [his] boyish days' with 'their glad animal movements' (74–5) and that time when, like the child during the stage of the 'semiotic *chora*', nature was

> An appetite: a feeling and a love,
> That had no need of a remoter charm,
> By thought supplied, or any interest
> Unborrowed from the eye. (81–4)

Wordsworth's 'use' of Dorothy in the poem (to return to the term used by John Barrell) is a continuation of this desire to establish a mature, adult and masculine poetic voice. It was noted earlier how Kristeva writes of the child's presence presenting an unsettling '*it*' into adult discourse: 'Reason was thus transcended by a *heterogeneous element* (biology: life) and by a *third party* (*I/you* communication is displaced by *it*: the child).'[32] Nature, and Wordsworth's always potentially 'childish' relationship with it, a relationship which forever challenges his sense of poetic adult (and masculine) identity is, to use Kristeva's term, an '*it*' which is translated within the poem into an unthreatening '*you*' (or, more correctly, 'thou') with the introduction of Dorothy:

> For thou art with me, here, upon the banks
> Of this fair river; thou, my dearest Friend
> My dear, dear Friend, and in thy voice I catch
> The language of my former heart ... (115–18)

It is on to Dorothy that the troubling pre-symbolic 'language' of Wordsworth's 'former heart' is placed: in asserting both his difference from and his control over his sister the poet is able to achieve the adult and masculine maturity that the poetic voice is striving for.

This chapter has attempted to show how, in both the linguistic and generic syntax of the poem, Wordsworth in 'Tintern Abbey' attempts to resist the perceived dangers of a 'feminised' discourse. There are a variety of ways in which such resistance could be understood. One might, for example, want to see it as typical of the phallocentric nature of Romanticism itself. One could also, however, set it within the context of the historical narrative constructed by David Simpson in his book *Romanticism, Nationalism and the Revolt Against Theory*. Simpson describes a tension he perceives to have existed during the so-called 'Romantic' period (and which still effectively exists in the present day) between 'theory', or rational thought, and the language of 'sensibility'. This tension is crucially figured by the language of gender:

On the one hand, theory and the analytic method were discredited as scientific and, sometimes, as dangerously democratic; on the other, a too complete complicity in the language of sensibility must render literature (and criticism) hyperfeminized, and thus culturally impotent and emotionally disabling.[33]

This chapter has demonstrated that, in certain circumstances, the 'feminine' could also be seen as politically dangerous and excessive. None the less, Simpson's point still holds for Wordsworth writing at the end of the 1790s: he desired a language that provided him with a meaningful public voice and yet the poetic traditions he was working within assumed a dependence upon the 'language of sensibility' which threatened to undermine such authority. By transferring the dangerously feminine 'language' of his 'former heart' on to Dorothy, the poet was able to accommodate the 'feminine' without allowing it to risk his overall 'masculine' control.

This masculine accommodation of the feminine can perhaps be interpreted as a compromise or an act of self-delusion or (far more seriously) an act of male oppression, but it can also be read rather

more positively. Discussing the often ambiguously gendered nature
of that category of writing called 'literature', Simpson observes that
'At times literature's very miscegenated identity has been made the
stuff of our salvation, as if, in a culture more and more defining itself
through extremes, the composite mode of literary response can be a
saving mixture.'[34] Approached in this way, 'Tintern Abbey' could be
said to reveal an ongoing attempt to explore the relationships
between social constructions of masculinity and femininity when
both were undergoing a process of radical transformation. No reso-
lutions are possible within the poem and, as I hope my analysis in the
present chapter has demonstrated, the full force of its dynamics can
only be recognised when its 'miscegenated' and 'composite' qualities
have been foregrounded. As I have shown, the genre of 'Tintern
Abbey' is similarly a decidedly 'composite mode' which reveals not
only a literary hesitancy but also an uncertainty regarding the possibility of a 'self' that can define itself through the 'extremes' of binarily opposed gender differences.

To appreciate that 'Tintern Abbey' is a generically unsettled text is
therefore central to a clear understanding of how it functions within
history; and to avoid its generic awkwardness is to evade some of its
most pervasive demands. In light of this, it is instructive to recon-
sider M.H. Abrams's influential attempt to define what he terms the
'Greater Romantic Lyric', a generic category in which he places not
only 'Tintern Abbey' but also Coleridge's 'Reflections on having left
a Place of Retirement'. Confronted with a group of poems which
appear to defy easy categorisation, Abrams's strategy is to suggest
that they represent the arrival of what is in effect a new genre: 'it was
the earliest Romantic formal invention, and at once demonstrated
the stability of organization and the capacity to engender successors
which define a distinct lyric species.'[35] Colluding with what Jerome
McGann has called the 'Romantic Ideology', Abrams here allows the
Romantic poets to define their own terms of reference: their poetry
becomes generically self-defining as a result. Abrams's tendency to
offer a linear and progressive narrative of genre development, underlined by his adoption of metaphors derived from biological evolu-
tion, can be related to Clifford Siskin's distinction between the
'history of genre' and a 'generic history'. For Siskin, a 'history of
genre' 'imposes a historical narrative on single forms, treating each
one as an independent, organic entity evolving naturally toward
greater sophistication. The result is usually a Romantic developmen-

tal tale such as *the* Novel's rise or *the* Lyric's flowering.'[36] Abrams's
notion of the 'Greater Romantic Lyric' clearly fits this description in
that, whilst it emerges as a 'new' form, it is also situated as the final
point in a 'developmental tale' ('it displaced what neoclassical critics
had called "the greater ode" – the elevated Pindaric, in distinction to
"the lesser ode" modelled chiefly on Horace – as the favoured form
for the long lyric poem').[37] Against 'the history of genre', Siskin
places the notion of 'generic history':

A generic history ... uses genre to construct history rather than the other
way round. Understood as a family concept, genre can address both
change *and* continuity, for it categorizes every text as a member both of
an ongoing kind and of a synchronically distinct set of relationships
among different kinds.[38]

Whilst my own approach in these first two chapters has queried the
extent to which the apparent deployment of a particular genre makes
an ultimately 'distinct' relationship with other genres possible, I
would agree with Siskin's insistence upon the use of genre analysis to
construct history. The ambiguities of Coleridge's pastoral in 'Reflections', and the oscillation between sonnet and ode in 'Tintern
Abbey', both allow the reader access to historical moments of doubt
and transition. However, Siskin also highlights the importance of a
diachronic relationship between the living writer and the community
of dead writers whose work remains to be read in the present. A consideration of such poetic influence is central to any discussion of
genre and has become, largely owing to the work of Harold Bloom,
a central concern of Romantic criticism. Poetic influence, and the
issues of gender and genre it gives rise to, are therefore an important
focus of the next chapter.

### NOTES

1 All references to Wordsworth's texts are taken from *William Wordsworth*
   (ed. Stephen Gill). Line numbers of quotations from poems are given in
   parentheses.
2 Barrell, *Poetry, Language and Politics*, pp.145–6. For a reading of 'Tintern
   Abbey' which also explores its depiction of gender and takes its starting
   point from Barrell's work, see John Williams, 'Wordsworth's "Tintern
   Abbey" in Context: Gender, Art and Romanticism'.
3 See Bourke, *Romantic Discourse and Political Modernity*, pp.40–57.
4 Todorov, *Genres in Discourse*, p.15.
5 Curran, *Poetic Form and British Romanticism*, pp.205–6.

6 See my discussion of McGann's *The Romantic Ideology* in the Introduction to the present book and, for a further discussion of the replication of 'Romantic Ideology' by twentieth-century critics (including McGann), Clifford Siskin, *The Historicity of Romantic Discourse*.

7 Todorov, *Genres in Discourse*, p.19.

8 The essay is to be found in Kristeva's *Desire in Language*, pp.271–94.

9 Jacobus, *Tradition and Experiment*, p.104.

10 Coleridge quoted from *Poems*, ed Beer; Warton quoted from *The New Oxford Book of Eighteenth-Century Verse*, ed. Lonsdale.

11 Curran, *Poetic Form and British Romanticism*, p.66.

12 Coleridge, *A Sheet of Sonnets* in *Complete Poetical Works*, p.1139.

13 Coleridge, *A Sheet of Sonnets*, p.1139.

14 Coleridge, *Biographia Literaria*, I.16–17.

15 See my discussion of Cixous's work in the Introduction.

16 Coleridge, *Biographia Literaria*, I.25.

17 Coleridge, *Selected Letters*, p.114.

18 Coleridge, *Biographia Literaria*, I.26.

19 Quoted in Mary Moorman, *William Wordsworth*, p.125.

20 See Moorman, *William Wordsworth*, p.170 and Stephen Gill, *William Wordsworth: A Life*, p.51 and p.57.

21 See Curran, *Poetic Form and British Romanticism*, p.39.

22 Kristeva, *Desire in Language*, p.284.

23 Kristeva, *Desire in Language*, p.286.

24 Wordsworth, *Letters*, pp.59–60.

25 It is instructive to place Wordsworth's account of Milton's sonnets in this letter alongside the comparison of the sublime and the beautiful in Burke's *Enquiry* which was discussed in the previous chapter: Milton's sonnets evidently provided Wordsworth with a 'sublime' alternative to the 'beautiful' ethos of the 'revisit' tradition.

26 Jacobus, *Tradition and Experiment*, p.114.

27 Kristeva, *Desire in Language*, p.271.

28 Kristeva, *Desire in Language*, p.276.

29 Kristeva, *Desire in Language*, p.276.

30 Kristeva, *Desire in Language*, p.287.

31 Kristeva, *Desire in Language*, p.288.

32 Kristeva, *Desire in Language*, p.271.

33 David Simpson, *Romanticism, Nationalism, and the Revolt Against Theory*, pp.151–2.

34 Simpson, *Romanticism, Nationalism*, p.152.

35 Abrams, 'Structure and Style in the Greater Romantic Lyric', originally published in 1965; quoted from *The Correspondent Breeze*, p.79.

36 Clifford Siskin, *The Historicity of Romantic Discourse*, p.10.

37 Abrams, *Correspondent Breeze*, pp.77–8.

38 Siskin, *The Historicity of Romantic Discourse*, p.10.

# 3
# William Wordsworth

## Genre and constructions
## of the 'self' in *The Prelude*

### I

To discuss *The Prelude* in the context of generic categorisation is
notoriously difficult for, whilst Wordsworth's long autobiographical
poem is usually read as some form of modified 'epic', it none the less
communicates to the reader a variety of conflicting generic signals. It
is tempting, for example, to read the poem as an important early contribution to the emerging generic form of the autobiography but this
might lead to a failure to register the fact that it can also be seen to
deploy a range of other generic modes including the pastoral, the ode,
the romance, the poetic epitaph and travel writing in addition to the
more obvious epic form. To add further to the difficulties, several
parts of *The Prelude* were published as separate poems in their own
right, thus suggesting that they could (and can) be read according to
different generic classifications.[1] In a persuasive reading of *The Prelude*'s depiction of Wordsworth's response to revolutionary France in
Books 9 and 10, Alan Liu writes of the fruitful and yet confusing 'pattern of generic turbulence' that characterises those books and, it could
be added, the poem as a whole.[2] If such 'generic turbulence' is what
defines the experience of reading *The Prelude*, and if the poem can be
seen as centrally autobiographical and thus concerned with definitions
of the self, then, by extension, one could suggest that this generic confusion is associated in some way with an equally disconcerting ontological doubt. Furthermore, such uncertainty about representations
of the 'self' can be related more precisely to the problems which sur-
round the construction and representation of a specifically 'masculine'
identity in the late eighteenth and early nineteenth centuries.

Such issues can be approached initially through a brief analysis of
a section from Book 1 where Wordsworth contemplates his poetic
vocation and indicates his awareness of certain hindrances to poetic
production:

> The Poet, gentle creature as he is,
> Hath, like the Lover, his unruly times -
> His fits when he is neither sick nor well,
> Though no distress be near him but his own
> Unmanageable thoughts. The mind itself,
> The meditative mind, best pleased perhaps
> While she as duteous as the mother dove
> Sits brooding, lives not always to that end,
> But hath less quiet instincts – goadings on
> That drives her as in trouble through the groves.
> With me is now such passion, which I blame
> No otherwise than as it lasts too long. (1.145–56)[3]

The nature of the 'poet' is here explicitly revealed as 'feminine', a man who is constituted by a typically 'unmanageable' force which partakes of both a reassuringly 'duteous' maternal aspect and also of a more passionate and disruptive element that makes use of 'less quiet instincts'. The poet's 'meditative mind', which, in the above passage at least, is seen as the centrally creative agent within the poet, is directly referred to as 'she': a fact which would point towards the 'feminine' nature of poetic creativity. Yet, of course, this apparently positive aspect of poetic femininity is only part of the story, for what Wordsworth is describing here is a period where poetic production is halted because of the poet's (necessary but troubling) 'unruly' fits. The feminine excesses of passionate feeling have lasted 'too long' and have distracted – and effectively seduced – the poet from the more productive task of poetic composition itself.

That Wordsworth feels his 'masculine' poetic persona to be threatened by this 'feminine' element is evident from the allusion to Milton's *Paradise Lost* which underlies his description of the poetic mind's dove-like 'brooding'. Milton describes the creation of matter out of original chaos in the same terms:

> thou from the first
> Wast present, and with mighty wings outspread
> Dove-like sat'st brooding on the vast abyss
> And madest it pregnant ... (1.19–22)

The initial effect of Wordsworth's allusion is to highlight the similarities between divine and poetic creation and thus to valorise the individual Romantic imagination; and yet, on further reflection, the reader is struck by the tensions established between the two texts and their respective authors. Whilst Milton might initially present his

god as a feminised 'brooding' figure, this depiction is quickly subsumed within an image of more explicitly 'masculine' sexuality as
chaos is made 'pregnant' by the creative virility of God the Father. In
Wordsworth's text, on the other hand, the image of the poetic mind
remains maternal and passive unless given to equally unproductive
'fits' of unruly feminine passion. Wordsworth's allusion, then, ultimately underlines his failure at this point in the poem to have created
anything and this failure is implicitly associated with the predominance of the 'feminine' within the poet.

As if in response to this (only half-acknowledged) doubt,
Wordsworth proceeds to give an account of his poetic endeavours in
a far more proactive and explicitly masculine guise:

> When, as becomes a man who would prepare
> For such a glorious work, I through myself
> Make rigorous inquisition, the report
> Is often chearing; for I neither seem
> To lack that first great gift, the vital soul,
> Nor general truths which are themselves a sort
> Of elements and agents, under-powers,
> Subordinate helpers of the living mind.
> Nor am I naked in external things,
> Forms, images, nor numerous other aids
> Of less regard, though won perhaps with toil,
> And needful to build up a poet's praise. (1.157–68)

In contrast with the earlier passage, the poetic self-definition here is
(almost too) self-evidently masculinist: Wordsworth depicts himself
as a hero who is about to embark upon an epic quest and deploys language and imagery which are implicitly martial in tone and implication. Against the passive maternal brooding of the earlier account,
Wordsworth offers a description of busy preparation; against the
frenzied and unproductive feminine 'passion', he presents action
which has a clear and deliberate focus where preparation itself is a
form of heroic activity in which various 'aids' have to be 'won …
with toil'.

This second passage, then, would seem to be written as an uneasy
response to the uncertainties revealed in the first and, in addition,
this response is conducted at one level in terms of generic taxonomy.
The allusion to Milton in the first passage reminds the reader of
Wordsworth's powerful masculine predecessor and establishes, as has
been noted, the discontinuities between Miltonic and Wordswor-

thian creativity at this point. Moreover, the allusion acts as a reminder of Milton's preeminence as an epic poet, a fact that would lead the reader to suspect that Wordsworth's 'heroic' discourse in the second passage is a response to his own perceived failure to match up to his poetic forefather's achievements in that genre. *The Prelude* is, after all, a poem which aims to portray 'the growth of the Poet's mind'[4] and the epic has traditionally been seen as, to quote Northrop Frye, 'the product of poetic maturity',[5] a belief humorously underlined by Coleridge's account of the preparation that would be necessary before he could embark upon his own epic poem:

I should not think of devoting less than 20 years to an Epic poem. Ten to collect materials, & warm my mind with universal Science – I would be a tolerable mathematician, I would thoroughly know mechanics, hydrostatics, optics, & Astronomy – Botany, Metallurgy, fossilism, chemistry, geology, Anatomy, Medicine, – then *the mind of man* – then *the minds of men* – in *all* Travels, Voyages & Histories. So would I spend ten years – the next five to the composition of the poem – & the last five to the correction of it.[6]

Despite the obvious humour here, Coleridge emphasises the fact that an epic poem should be thought of as a product of poetic maturity and also that it should be conceived as a public genre which engages with active (masculine) social identity. This is something to which Wordsworth draws the reader's attention when he refers to the necessary coupling of his own 'vital soul' (compare the virile agency of Milton's creative deity) with 'external things' which are a prerequisite for a successful epic. He further stresses that the domain of the epic is a public, and therefore necessarily masculine, one where the successful poet is rewarded with hard-won 'praise'.

To spend so long discussing Wordsworth's epic aspirations is not to deny the other competing generic modes that were cited earlier, nor is it necessarily to claim a priority for the epic mode. Rather, this section of *The Prelude* has been dwelt upon to illustrate how generic choice is intimately related to questions of self-definition and to argue that both of these aspects of the poem are dependent upon a consideration of the construction and representation of gender. Tzvetan Todorov has argued that '[g]enres are precisely those relay-points by which the work assumes a relation with the universe of literature'.[7] In the sections from *The Prelude* examined so far, it could be said that Wordsworth is using generic markers to map out his relationship with Milton in the 'universe of literature' but it could also be claimed that Wordsworth's 'mapping' extends beyond 'literature' and relates to the 'universe' of social identity. Wordsworth uses genre, and its inherent gender distinctions, to explore his own construction of a 'masculine' self: an appeal to the apparent certainties of genre classification seemingly defers doubt about gender classifications. The function of genre, from this perspective, becomes a conservative one which attempts to fix that which is in constant danger of escaping clearly defined taxonomies. It is to this aspect of genre theory that Mary Jacobus directs her attention:

> Is genre theory ... a means of stabilizing the errant text by putting a face on it, and so reading into it a recognizable, specular image of our own acts of understanding? In this light, theories of genre become inseparable from theories of the subject, and hence inseparable from theories of writing.[8]

The aim of the present chapter is to build upon the observations of Todorov and Jacobus cited above by adopting a methodology derived from psychoanalytic criticism which makes possible further analysis of the relationships between genre theory and the construction of a gendered self. Todorov's 'universe of literature' which genre provides access to can be likened to that other, earlier, universe of signification – the Symbolic and the Name of the Father – thus relating issues of genre more directly to initial constructions of a separate 'self'. Jacobus's suggestive description of genre as a 'specular image of our own acts of understanding' intimates a certain narcissistic component in the deployment of genre classification which can usefully be read against Sigmund Freud's notions of narcissism and Julia Kristeva's development of them. It is hoped, then, that a psychoanalytic approach to the question of genre in relation to *The Prelude* will reveal the difficulties inherent in representing a stable, knowable and 'readable' self in the late eighteenth and early nineteenth centuries. However, before moving on to the insights to be gained from Freud and Kristeva, it is necessary to consider in slightly more detail the question of poetic and generic influence through a discussion of the influential ideas of Harold Bloom.

## II

In his book *The Anxiety of Influence*, Harold Bloom outlines a 'theory of poetry' which defines literary history in terms of the relationship between the contemporary poet and his (never really, in Bloom's work, her) poetic predecessors or 'precursors': 'Poetic history, in this book's argument, is held to be indistinguishable from poetic influence, since strong poets make that history by misreading one another, so as to clear imaginative space for themselves.'[9] The 'strong poet' attempts to defeat the 'anxiety' of being influenced by an earlier poet by offering a creative misreading or act of 'misprision' in his own work through which he strives to overcome his feeling of belatedness and assert his own poetic maturity. In his exposition of this theory of influence, Bloom draws explicitly upon the work of Sigmund Freud to provide a model for the relationships he is describing:

Poetic influence, or as I shall more frequently term it, poetic misprision, is necessarily the study of the poet-as-poet. When such a study considers the context in which that life-cycle is enacted, it will be compelled to examine simultaneously the relations between poets as cases akin to what Freud called the family romance, and as chapters in the history of modern revisionism, 'modern' meaning here post-Enlightenment.[10]

The 'strong poets' that Bloom presents his reader with are writers who enter into a fraught contest with their poetic forefathers in a version of Freud's Oedipal conflict where sons desire the deaths of their fathers in order to establish their own (masculine) identity: 'My concern is only with strong poets, major figures with the persistence to wrestle with their precursors, even to the death'.[11]

Whilst Bloom's theories of influence draw upon Freudian analogies in the ways outlined above, it is not the case that Bloom presents his analysis as literally psychoanalytic: he is not concerned with the mental processes of the poet as a specific human being in a specific social context but rather, as he says, with the 'poet-as-poet'. Peter de Bolla observes that

the anxiety we turn our attention to in the Bloomian theory of influence – the attention we pay to poetic misprision – was never internal to an individual but always the province of the poem itself. In this way, Bloom's theory, whatever it may on occasion look like, is not about individuals but about texts, about poems.[12]

Thus, when Bloom writes of 'history' he is primarily interested in a narrowly defined literary history, what Todorov terms the 'universe of literature' rather than a broader 'universe' of socially interactive individuals. None the less, in his use of a psychoanalytical model, Bloom has inevitably constructed a theory which impinges upon issues of sexuality and gender – even if these issues are effectively ignored by Bloom himself. Sandra Gilbert and Susan Gubar, on the other hand, foreground the social and sexual politics of Bloom's critical position when they engage with the notion of literary influence in relation to women writers of the nineteenth century in *The Madwoman in the Attic*: 'Bloom's model of literary history is intensely (even exclusively) male, and necessarily patriarchal. For this reason it has seemed, and no doubt will continue to seem, offensively sexist to some feminist critics.'[13] Rather than criticising or objecting to Bloom's ideas on these grounds, however, Gilbert and Gubar stress the importance and relevance of his work as an aid to an understanding of the forces at play within western cultural traditions:

For Western literary history *is* overwhelmingly male – or, more accurately, patriarchal – and Bloom analyses and explains this fact, while other theorists have ignored it, precisely, one supposes, because they assumed that literature had to be male. Like Freud, whose psychoanalytic postulates permeate Bloom's literary psychoanalyses of the 'anxiety of influence', Bloom has defined processes of interaction that his predecessors did not bother to consider because, amongst other reasons, they were themselves so caught up in such processes. Like Freud, too, Bloom has insisted on bringing to consciousness assumptions readers and writers do not ordinarily examine. In doing so, he has clarified the implications of the psychosexual and sociosexual con-texts by which every literary text is surrounded.[14]

Whilst such a critique of Bloom's work enables Gilbert and Gubar to position it within a social context – and permits them to define and explore the very different 'anxieties' and 'influences' that are at work within the writings of women authors – it leaves unquestioned the validity of his fundamental assumption that, if a psychoanalytical model for literary influence is adopted, then the most suitable analogy is that provided by the Oedipal scenario.[15]

It was noted earlier how Mary Jacobus describes the deployment of genre theory as a means of establishing a 'specular image of our own acts of understanding' and it was suggested that this kind of self-validating or self-reflective activity could be related to notions of narcissism, primary narcissism being, according to Freud, a pre-Oedipal trait: 'We say that the human being originally has two sexual objects: himself and the woman who tends him, and thereby we postulate a primary narcissism in everyone, which may in the long run manifest itself as dominating his object choice.'[16] If one attempts to reinterpret theories of influence through a model founded upon ideas of narcissism, therefore, the effect will be to challenge Bloom's insistence upon the primacy of male competitiveness and mutual male 'anxiety' and to resituate the debate within the arena of the mother–child relationship. Freud works towards an understanding of narcissism through a series of hypotheses which invite direct comparison with Romantic depictions of the poet and the poetic imagination and thus suggest the relevance of his ideas for a clearer understanding of the processes at work within Romantic texts. His construction of what 'primary narcissism' might be like, for example, is founded upon his observation of the ways in which its traces reveal themselves in subsequent manifestations. He directs his reader's attention in particular to the behavioural patterns of 'primitive peoples' and children:

In the former we find characteristics which, if they occurred singly, might be put down to megalomania: an over-estimation of the power of wishes and mental processes, the 'omnipotence of thoughts', a belief in the magic virtue of words, and a method of dealing with the outer world – the art of 'magic' – which appears to be a logical application of these grandiose premises. In the child of our own day, whose development is much more obscure to us, we expect a perfectly analogous attitude toward the external world.[17]

In this double analogy, Freud presents a depiction of narcissism which parallels Romantic preoccupation with the primitive and childlike. Many of the poems in *Lyrical Ballads*, for instance, demonstrate Wordsworth's interest in both of these areas, as is revealed, in different ways, in poems such as 'Goody Blake and Harry Gill' (with its examination of 'the power of wishes and mental processes' and 'the magic virtue of words') or 'We are Seven' (which demonstrates a version of childish 'megalomania' in the child's refusal to accommodate an adult awareness of death). Yet to dwell simply upon literal accounts of the primitive and child-like in Wordsworth's poetry is to ignore the ways in which the 'megalomania' located by Freud in relation to narcissism is apposite to a broader understanding of the Romantic belief in the power of imagination. As Wordsworth himself says of his intentions in writing 'Goody Blake and Harry Gill', for example: 'I wished to draw attention to the truth, that the power of the human imagination is sufficient to produce such changes even in our physical nature as might almost appear miraculous.'[18] For Wordsworth (and the other Romantic poets) a belief in the 'magic virtue of words' was a crucial part of their imaginative creed (even if it was inevitably constantly beset by undermining doubts) and one can therefore suggest that what has often been termed Romantic 'egotism' can be understood through an application of Freud's narrative of a primary narcissism and its residual effects.

Having applied Freud's ideas thus far, however, one could progress further and propose that his ideas also provide an initial model for a theory of Romantic 'influence', particularly in relation to the use of earlier generic modes. Freud develops his initial supposition of the two initial 'sexual objects' into a consideration of adult love and proposes that a person may love according to two 'types': the 'anaclitic', which relates to the primary love for the person who nurtures; and the 'narcissistic'. According to the 'narcissistic type', a person may love:

(a) What he is himself (actually himself).
(b) What he once was.
(c) What he would like to be.
(d) Someone who was once part of himself.[19]

One can see from this that Wordsworth's evocation of Milton, for example, could be seen as a narcissistic self-projection in terms of 'what he would like to be'. Rather than a father-figure who is there to be confronted as a stern and admonitory other, Milton is subjugated to Wordsworth's own self-presentation: he becomes, to adapt Jacobus's phrase, 'a *textual* image of *Wordsworth*'s own (*self*) understanding'. (Indeed, Freud's model of narcissistic love could be applied to *The Prelude* as a whole: it is an autobiographical poem ('what he is himself') largely about the poet's own childhood and youth ('what he once was') which aspires to bring the poet public acclaim ('what he would like to be') and which is addressed to his close friend Coleridge (who, it could be claimed, was 'someone who was once part of himself'.))

It might be objected here, none the less, that this account of narcissism does little to explain the sense of guidance or instruction which is often associated with a poetic predecessor who is acknowledged as an 'influence'. Here again, however, Freud's theories offer an explanatory framework in their depiction of what Freud terms the 'ego ideal':

The narcissism seems now to be displaced on to this new ideal ego, which, like the infantile ego, deems itself the possessor of all perfections. As always where the libido is concerned, here again man has shown himself incapable of giving up a gratification he has once enjoyed. He is not willing to forgo his narcissistic perfection in his childhood; and if, as he develops, he is disturbed by the admonitions of others and his own critical judgement is awakened, he seeks to recover the early perfection, thus wrested from him, in the new form of an ego-ideal. That which he projects ahead of him as his ideal is merely his substitute for the lost narcissism of his childhood – the time when he was his own ideal.[20]

Seen in these terms, Milton becomes one aspect of the 'ideal ego' that Wordsworth constructs in *The Prelude*, a figure who is there as a perfection to be emulated but also a perfection which at a crucial level stands in for the narcissistic goal of a libidinous desire. Wordsworth's relationship with Milton within the poem, therefore, becomes not so much a struggle for poetic maturity defined in terms of an Oedipal clash where success brings the poet into what might be termed the Symbolic but, rather, it is a manifestation of a pre-Oedipal desire, namely a primary narcissism, which has found an alternative vehicle for its expression. As Freud writes later in the same essay:

The development of the ego consists in a departure from the primary narcissism and results in a vigorous attempt to recover it. This departure is brought about by means of the displacement of the libido to an ego-ideal imposed from without, while gratification is derived from the attainment of this ideal.[21]

While Milton might be an external agent, effectively 'imposed from without' through the processes of cultural education and expectations he can also therefore be seen as a vehicle for Wordsworth's own narcissistic self-gratification.

More recently, Julia Kristeva has developed Freud's ideas on narcissism in order to relate them more directly to the formation of a sense of 'self' in the pre-Oedipal domain. She takes as her starting point the fact that, as Freud maintained, the origins of primary narcissism are dependent upon some kind of 'new action' which supplements the original 'mother–child dyad' and enables the child to gain a sense of him- or herself as a separate entity. In order to explain this new departure, one which causes the initial rupture between child and mother and which, therefore, anticipates entry into the Symbolic and the Name of the Father, Kristeva makes what at first appears to be a surprising intellectual leap: 'It prompts one to conceive of an

archaic paternal function, preceding the Name, the Symbolic ... a
disposition that one might call that of the imaginary father.'[22] This
'imaginary father' is not an actual father, nor is 'he' actually gendered:
indeed he does not literally exist as an 'object' for the child. He is,
rather, an entity that is perceived by the child as an 'object of desire'
for the mother and it is this perception by the child that initiates the
divorce from the mother in her role as simply a source of auto-erotic
satisfaction. The 'imaginary father' becomes a necessary 'other' for
both child and mother:

She will love her child with respect to that Other, and it is through a discourse aimed at that Third Party that the child will be set up as 'loved' for
the mother. 'Isn't he beautiful', or 'I am proud of you', and so forth, are
statements of maternal love because they involve a Third Party; it is in
the eyes of a Third Party that the baby a mother speaks to becomes a he.[23]

The mother's terms of endearment are thus diverted via the imagined
presence of the 'imaginary father', and it is the validating perspective
of this imaginary figure that enables the child to form a primary sense
of its existence beyond the mother–child relationship.

Central to Kristeva's discussion of narcissism is her analysis of
'amatory identification' which she explores through the notion of
'Einfühlung' or the assimilation of other people's feelings. She notes
that the state of being in love is dependent upon a sense of self-identification with the object of one's affections, and relates this phenomenon to the 'oral phase of the libido's organization where what
I incorporate is what I become'.[24] Love, then, is ultimately an emotion founded upon a quasi-narcissistic impulse which relies upon a
sense of 'reduplication': 'I identify, not with an object, but with what
offers itself to me as a *model*. That enigmatic apprehending of a *pattern* to be imitated ... leads us to wonder whether the loving state is
a state without an object and reminds us of an archaic *reduplication*
(rather than imitation).'[25] One can begin to see here how Kristeva's
theories of the narcissistic foundation of 'love' can be related to theories of 'influence' where the contemporary poet looks back to the
work of a predecessor which 'offers itself ... as a *model*' and as a '*pattern* to be imitated'. In both cases it is a process of 'identification'
which establishes a sense of 'self' in terms of a self-reflection in the
'other'. She further notes that her theories of 'identification' have a
particular resonance when applied to the realm of 'what constitutes
man's being, namely *language*. When the object that I incorporate is

the speech of the other – precisely a non-object, a pattern, a model – I bind myself to him in a primary fusion, communion, unification. An identification.'[26] Later in her essay Kristeva re-emphasises the importance of her understanding of love for the formation and consolidation of a knowable and stable sense of 'self': 'The object of love is a metaphor for the subject – its constitutive metaphor, its "unary feature".'[27] Love is founded upon a primary narcissism, then, and this original narcissistic urge reveals itself in later manifestations of love. Both love and narcissism are related to the creation and maintenance of identity and protect the self against the encroachment of potential chaos which is initially revealed within the pre-Oedipal situation when the first separation between mother and child is brought about by an awareness of the 'imaginary father':

Narcissism protects emptiness, ensures an elementary separation. Without that solidarity between emptiness and narcissism, chaos would sweep away any possibility of distinction, trace and symbolization, which would in turn confuse the limits of the body, words, the real and the symbolic.[28]

Seen in these terms, therefore, the use of generic models derived from poetic predecessors can be read according to two related impulses: the first is the desire to confirm an acceptable and discrete construction of the 'self' by (seemingly paradoxically) 'incorporating' the work of another as a 'pattern' or 'model' which enables a sense (self) identification to be represented; the second is a corresponding need to protect the 'emptiness' which inevitably underlies and threatens to undermine any such construction of self-identity – as Kristeva notes early in her essay, 'narcissism … reveals itself as a screen over *emptiness*'.[29]

This section has attempted to outline Harold Bloom's theories of poetic influence which rely upon a revised version of Freud's notions of an Oedipal conflict between fathers and sons for their sense of the dynamics of literary history. In place of such Oedipal struggle it has been suggested that both Freud's speculations concerning a primary narcissism and Kristeva's reworkings of them can be used as an alternative model of influence which derives its impetus from the pre-Oedipal arena and thus allows the critic to focus upon the crises of self-identification which take place when the subject prepares to enter the realm of the Symbolic and the patriarchal Name of the Father and, perhaps more importantly, also makes possible an exploration of

those residual drives and fears which haunt the child after his or her
departure from the mother–child dyad. What remains to be
attempted in the remainder of this chapter is an analysis of the ways
in which such theoretical frameworks can aid an understanding of
*The Prelude* and Wordsworth's strategies for the construction of a
stable masculine identity within that text.

### III

In Book 5 of *The Prelude*, Wordsworth includes a now famous
account of a boy from the Lake District who amuses himself by com-
municating with owls through the production of 'mimic hootings'.
It is an account which becomes particularly interesting when placed
in the context of primary narcissism and Kristeva's observations
upon it.

> There was a boy – ye knew him well, ye cliffs
> And islands of Winander – many a time
> At evening, when the stars had just begun
> To move along the edges of the hills,
> Rising or setting, would he stand alone
> Beneath the trees or by the glimmering lake,
> And there, with fingers interwoven, both hands
> Pressed closely palm to palm, and to his mouth
> Uplifted, he as through an instrument
> Blew mimic hootings to the silent owls
> That they might answer him. And they would shout
> Across the wat'ry vale, and shout again,
> Responsive to his call, with quivering peals
> And long halloos, and screams, and echoes loud,
> Redoubled and redoubled – concourse wild
> Of mirth and jocund din. (5.389–404)

In his use of his voice as 'an instrument' with which to sing, the boy
here, as several critics have noted, becomes a type for the poet and,
as such, it is significant that his poetic discourse should be founded
upon the notion of mimicry. In establishing his own poetic voice, the
poet looks for other voices that can be imitated – he looks for an earlier poet who can serve, to use Kristeva's terms, as a 'pattern' or a
'model'. The boy-poet 'incorporates' the 'speech' of the owls in order
to establish a sense of self through a unifying process of 'identification'. Furthermore it should be noted how, in this passage, although

the boy is seen to establish a relationship with the owls based on his own mimicry of their 'hootings', it is the boy himself who initiates the exchange: the owls are initially 'silent' and are only provoked into 'speech' through the child's own 'language'. Thus, when the owls do eventually respond to his advances, their own 'voices' ironically appear to be mimicking the boy's own mimicry and so, through an original act of mimicry, the child's own voice seems to gain a certain primacy and therefore apparent authenticity. This assertion of his own poetic 'voice' eventually leads to a process of unification where the boy's song is confirmed through its reverberation throughout the landscape as a series of 'echoes' which 'redoubled and redoubled'. This redoubling, which can be related to an amatory identification founded upon a primary narcissism, recalls what Kristeva terms the 'reduplication' that is necessary for the emergence of the subject's own identity:

As magnet of identification constitutive of identity and condition for that unification, which ensures the advent of the subject for an object, the 'object' of *Einfühlung* is a *metaphorical* object. Carrying auto-erotic motility to the unifying image of One Agency that already sets me up as an opposite One is the zero degree of subjectivity.[30]

As a 'metaphor' for the poetic self the owls provide the boy-poet with an 'object' which enables the 'zero degree of subjectivity' to emerge. Read in terms of theories of genre and poetic influence in general, the poets and poetic models who are the 'objects' of 'mimicry' and 'identification' allow the poet's own voice to come into being via a process which, to modify Kristeva's formulation, 'sets the poet up as an opposite One'.

Wordsworth's account of the boy of Winander does not end here, though, for he proceeds to introduce a more troubling note into his narrative:

> And when it chanced
> That pauses of deep silence mocked his skill,
> Then sometimes in that silence, while he hung
> Listening, a gentle shock of mild surprize
> Has carried far into his heart the voice
> Of mountain torrents; or the visible scene
> Would enter unawares into his mind
> With all its solemn imagery, its rocks,
> Its woods, and that uncertain heaven, received
> Into the bosom of the steady lake. (5.404–13)

One could claim here that the 'silence' experienced by the child is analogous to the 'emptiness' which is for Kristeva 'screened' by narcissism. There is an interesting reversal of the boy's and owls' actions in this section of the poem for, whereas initially the birds appear in their hootings to imitate the voice that calls to them, here the boy effectively reproduces the silence that the birds initiate. The tables are turned on the child as the birds replace mimicry with mockery where 'mockery' also hints at its secondary definition of 'imitation' (cf. Shelley in 'Ozymandias': 'The hand that mocked them').[31] The birds thus remind the child (by reproducing it) of the 'silence' or 'emptiness' of which he is constituted beneath the 'screen' of his narcissistic 'identification' with an 'other' which enables him to constitute a sense of 'self'. The result of this confrontation with silence and emptiness is a state of confusion which Kristeva was earlier recorded as describing as one where 'chaos [sweeps] away any possibility of distinction ... which ... in turn confuse[s] the limits of the body, words, the real and the symbolic'.[32] What emerges is not a mirroring of internal and external, self and other, but a confusion of boundaries where the 'voice / Of Mountain torrents' penetrates the child's body and the boy is passively 'unaware' of the ways in which he is defined against those forces which had appeared before to be separate entities. The whole intercourse becomes one which is as uncertain as the 'uncertain heaven' which is mirrored on the surface of the 'steady lake'. However, lest the reader should assume that this final image of mirroring is a return to a more certain narcissism, the text describes it in terms of an act of appropriation:

> that uncertain heaven, received
> Into the bosom of the steady lake.

One could suggest of the passage as a whole that, initially at least, the owls play the part of a 'third Party' (the imaginary father) which enables the child to break free from the potential restrictions of the mother–child dyad. Here, at the end of the section, the way in which the lake receives the landscape into its all-encompassing 'bosom' suggests a return to the maternal body as the controlling force which, on its own, denies the emergence of 'self'. As Kristeva notes: 'without the maternal "diversion" towards a Third Party, the bodily exchange is abjection or devouring.'[33] This denial of self effectively implies the figurative death of a distinct identity, a figurative trope which the narrative of the boy of Winander renders into literal event:

> This boy was taken from his mates, and died
> In childhood ere he was full ten years old. (5.414–15)

Metaphorically received into the bosom of the (maternal) lake, the boy drowns in a watery grave of ontological indeterminacy.

In more general terms – or, at least, in terms which are perhaps more familiar to students of Romanticism – Wordsworth reveals to the reader through this story of the boy of Winander the threat to personal autonomy presented by an apparently all-powerful, and feminised, 'Nature'. Margaret Homans has argued in *Women Writers and Poetic Identity* that 'When Mother Nature and other feminine figures are objectified as the other, they may be possessed or become the property of the subject.'[34] Whilst it is true that in the present episode nature is presented as 'maternal' and, at one level, distinctly 'other' than the boy-poet, it is quite clearly not the case that this version of nature can be possessed by the subject – indeed, it has been shown that the very existence of this 'subject' is problematised by the feminine force revealed through the landscape. Wordsworth's presentation of nature here is not so much a demonstration of masculine power as a declaration of the residual hold the maternal body has over the poet. In order for an autonomous self to emerge it is necessary for there to be a Third Party – what Kristeva calls the 'imaginary father' – and which the present analysis has related to the role played by the owls in the present episode or, more generally, to the function played by previous poets who offer themselves as 'patterns' or 'models' for the new poet's 'mimic' voice. Unlike the 'real' father, however, the 'imaginary' father represented by the owls does not reveal itself to be in violent opposition to 'mother nature' – in fact it almost appears to be part of it which is in keeping with the rather vague and nebulous character of this entity as described by Kristeva. Kristeva, it should be remembered, states quite clearly that the 'imaginary father' is neither male nor female, masculine nor feminine, and, therefore, whilst this figure enables an escape from the child-mother dyad and anticipates entry into the Symbolic and Oedipal conflict, it does not generate the same male tyranny as the real father who is yet to come. What Wordsworth offers initially, then, is a vision of the emergence of a sense of self which is not dependent upon a subjugation of the 'feminine' to a 'masculine' control and where poetic 'influence' can be seen as wholly enabling rather than being based upon an ultimately self-destructive Oedipal struggle.

The section which follows on immediately from Wordsworth's
account of the boy of Winander is not entirely clear as to its purpose
but, in that it introduces a discussion of the relevance of books for
the developing mind, its themes are clearly related to the issues currently under consideration. Wordsworth moves from his focus upon
the child who has died to mention those children still alive and then
on to thoughts of his own childhood:

> We might have fed upon a fatter soil
> Of Arts and Letters, but be that forgiven -
> A race of real children, not too wise,
> Too learned, or too good, but wanton, fresh,
> And bandied up and down by love and hate;
> Fierce, moody, patient, venturous, modest, shy,
> Mad at their sports like withered leaves in the winds;
> Though doing wrong and suffering, and full oft
> Bending beneath our life's mysterious weight
> Of pain and fear, yet still in happiness
> Not yielding to the happiest upon earth.
> Simplicity in habit, truth in speech,
> Be these the daily strengtheners of their minds!
> May books and Nature be their early joy,
> And knowledge, rightly honored with that name -
> Knowledge not purchased with the loss of power! (5.434–49)

In many ways this passage could be said to be confused – not least in
the way in which it opens by apparently rejecting the agency of
books and yet concludes by recommending it. Having said this, these
very confusions could be said to inform the reader of certain tensions
and uncertainties within the text. Wordsworth begins by dismissing
the need for the artificially enriched soil of 'Arts and Letters' in favour
of the more 'natural' environment in which he grew up, an environment which encourages an implicit sense of freedom and, it is
claimed, a true feeling of happiness. Yet this freedom could also be
described as a form of inconstancy or unpredictability, it is a state
where conflicting emotions are seen to co-exist – the boys are at once
'fierce, moody, patient, venturous, modest, shy' – and therefore a
state which might appear to challenge any notion of a stable 'self'.
Indeed, one might liken this apparently enviable condition to that
which generated the 'unmanageable thoughts' of the feminised poet
discussed earlier who revealed his poetic nature, as the children reveal
the essence of their childhood, through his 'unruly times' (1.149). As

the passage progresses, however, this emphasis upon the 'unruly' becomes less evident and a certain sobriety takes over:

> Simplicity in habit, truth in speech,
> Be these the daily strengtheners of their minds!

As this process reaches its climax, Wordsworth reintroduces the subject of books which are now seen as a necessary counterbalance to the potential excesses of 'Nature': 'May books and Nature be their early joy'. If 'nature' is seen as a feminised presence in *The Prelude*, then books, which are here established in terms of a binary opposition, are gendered as masculine: Wordsworth presents a gendered opposition between nature and culture where culture, here in the form of poetry, is able to 'possess' and contain the power of its feminised 'other'. In place of the earlier engagement with issues of self, gender, 'nature' and 'culture' which could be seen to relate to a potentially more liberating interaction between the different forces, Wordsworth here falls back on to more commonplace gender categorisations. The same is true if we relate the development of the passage to a consideration of theories of influence and genre. Because he reinscribes masculinity into his presentation of 'books', Wordsworth implicitly reestablishes a model of writing which is effectively determined by a masculine desire for control of a feminine 'other' (in this case 'Nature') and, by implication, reintroduces a notion of literary influence as the arena for masculine competition.

## IV

The mode of argument so far adopted by the present chapter might be accused of being an example of what Tilottama Rajan, in an essay entitled 'The Erasure of Narrative in Post-Structuralist Representations of Wordsworth', has termed 'paradigmatism'.[35] Taking just one episode from *The Prelude*, there has been an apparent tendency to read this isolated passage as a 'paradigm' of the poem in its entirety without bringing into consideration the ways in which it relates to other sections of the text, particularly its immediate context(s). What remains to be attempted in the rest of this chapter is the reinstatement of the boy of Winander episode into *The Prelude* as a whole and a discussion of the ways in which its situation within the larger context of the poem modifies its significance and offers a way of returning to the larger generic issues raised at the beginning of the chapter.

It is evident from the title of Rajan's essay that her objection to 'paradigmatism' is based upon her sense that it ignores the 'narrative' element within Wordsworth's texts and thus it is an objection which can be seen to relate directly and explicitly to questions of genre. Rajan detects a trend within twentieth-century Wordsworth criticism which valorises the 'lyric' element at the expense of the 'narrative' and, as a result, misrepresents the complex nature of the poetry and its constructions of a sense of 'self'. As she writes in another essay on a closely related topic:

pure lyric is a monologic form, where narrative and drama alike are set in the space of difference. The latter present the self in interaction with other characters and events. But lyric, as a purely subjective form, is marked by the exclusion of the other through which we become aware of the difference of the self from itself.[36]

In this earlier essay, Rajan engages specifically with the boy of Winander episode in terms of the inherent tensions it reveals between the 'lyric' and the 'narrative'. She notes that lines 389-413 were published separately by Wordsworth and therefore were required to be read, in that context, as a discrete lyric poem whilst their inclusion within the larger narrative space of The Prelude invited a modification of this original reading. As a lyric, she sug-gests, the poem is one which celebrates a visionary moment of com-munion with nature and the achievement of a unified self; as part of a narrative poem, on the other hand, which introduces the passing of time and the 'fact' of the child's death, the passage needs to be read differently. She observes that the lines which record the child's death force the reader

to re-read what has just been said by shifting our frame of reference from a lyric one, in which we consent to the suspension of time, to a narrative frame, in which we read the text to discover what has happened, what has changed. In other words, they disturb the closure of a poem which previously had been sealed against afterthoughts.[37]

Ironically, given her later views on 'paradigmatism', Rajan proceeds to read this episode within the text as a paradigm for Wordsworth's poetic practice in The Prelude as a whole: 'Wordsworth's decision to absorb "There was a boy" into The Prelude is a paradigm for what happens throughout the prehistory of the longer poem, as the still unwritten lyrical voice is situated in the prose of the world.'[38] In psychoanalytic terms, Rajan's definitions of 'lyric' and 'narrative' might here be mapped on to the Lacanian distinction between the 'Imaginary' (where the child perceives no distinction between him/herself and the outside world) and the 'Symbolic' (which is structured according to a series of differences).

Whilst this discussion of the boy of Winander episode in terms of generic shifts is interesting and apposite, it fails to take into consideration certain important aspects of the text. Firstly, even as a lyric, the poem contains its own uncertainties which threaten the presentation of a stable 'self' divorced from notions of 'difference': indeed, it has been suggested that the emergence of a sense of self is predicated upon an awareness of such differences and that it is the erasure of difference which leads to the demise of the self. Secondly, it presupposes a clear distinction between 'lyric' and 'narrative' which the text itself fails to uphold: the supposedly 'lyric' poem 'There was a boy' has its own (mini-)narrative to tell and possesses at least two distinct stages or episodes (firstly the child's 'mimic hootings' being responded to by the owls and, secondly, the owls' silent response and the boy's troubled reaction). Having made these objections, however, a modified version of Rajan's generic distinction between lyric and narrative strategies can still usefully be applied to the present discussion.

Lyric and narrative could be said to relate to two different constructions of the self as depicted in the boy of Winander episode. Lyric denotes a sense of self which is reliant upon a process of unification where the 'self' finds itself through a narcissistic mirroring in a perceived 'other' – this would be analogous to the first stage of the section from *The Prelude* where the boy's 'mimicry' works to confirm his own identity. This sense of a self which is rooted in a narcissistic self-identification responds to the 'closure' and apparent erasure of difference that Rajan observes in lyric poetry. Narrative, on the other hand, constructs a version of the self which is founded upon an awareness of difference both in relation to others and to the self itself as it changes in relation to the processes of time. Narrative, therefore, introduces a mode where lines of demarcation have to be rigorously established and protected (protagonists need to be clearly differentiated) and where the presence of time brings an implicit knowledge of death. Although, as has been seen, narrative is present throughout the boy of Winander episode, Rajan is therefore right to stress its presence in the section where Wordsworth situates the boy in relation to the village community as a whole and also informs the reader of his death.

In terms of the passage under consideration, then, the 'lyric' impulse can be described as narcissistic and pre-Oedipal whereas the 'narrative' drive can be referred to as an Oedipal one which relies upon a notion of identity through the maintenance of difference. Narrative resituates the lyric within the world (as Rajan says) and also, in the present example, resituates it within what Todorov calls the 'universe of literature' through its advocacy of the importance of 'books' for a child's social and spiritual development. It was argued in the previous section that Wordsworth's recourse to books here signals a return to what one might term the Bloomian model of influence, one which is based upon a masculine control of residual uncertainties remaining from the mother–child dyad. As *The Prelude* becomes a narrative poem modelled upon (and yet in competition with) Miltonic epic, its lyric moments, which foreground a different kind of self-knowledge not founded upon such masculine self-assertion in the face of difference, are subsumed within a genre which provides access to a patriarchal literary tradition and, implicitly, a patriarchal society.

However, this is not the whole story. In their critique of Bloom's theory of influence, Gilbert and Gubar note that his work should be read not as advocating a patriarchal society but as revealing the ways in which such a society – and its literary traditions – work. In her development of Freud's work on primary narcissism, Kristeva notes how the 'imaginary father' paves the way for what she terms the 'ulterior, unavoidable Oedipal destiny' where the child will enter the Symbolic and the Name of the Father.[39] If one applies a version of Gilbert and Gubar's critique to Kristeva one could argue that her work reveals a state of affairs which is not an inevitability. And, if this is so, then her account of the 'imaginary father' can be seen, in her own terms, to offer a source of hope for a different future:

Maintaining against the winds and high tides of our modern civilization the requirement of a stern father who, through his Name, brings about separation, judgement and identity, constitutes a necessity, a more or less pious wish. But we can only note that if this sternness is shaken, far from leaving us orphaned or inexorably psychotic, such an unsettling action will reveal multiple and varied destinies for paternity – notably of archaic, imaginary paternity. These destinies could or can be manifested by the clan as a whole.[40]

In the face of what appears to be an unavoidable certainty, Kristeva offers a vision of a potentially different masculinity, one which is dependent upon a residual awareness of the imaginary father who allows the development of an autonomous self from within the mother–child dyad. In a similar way one could claim that Wordsworth's description of the boy of Winander offers a potentially new and liberating vision of the poet's relationship not only with nature and the 'feminine' but also with his (or her) poetic predecessors. In terms of patriarchal structures, Wordsworth's evocation of a pre-Oedipal possibility might be seen as a failure of the 'masculine' self to enter fully into the Symbolic and the Name of the Father that primary narcissism is usually assumed to anticipate. In terms of an alternative version of poetic influence which eschews notions of masculine rivalry this very failure could be seen as a success.

## NOTES

1 See Tilottama Rajan, 'Romanticism and the Death of Lyric Consciousness', for an interesting discussion of one example of this which will be returned to at the end of the present chapter.
2 Alan Liu, ' "Shapeless Eagerness": The Genre of Revolution in Books 9–10 of *The Prelude*', p.6.
3 The edition of *The Prelude* used throughout is *The Prelude 1799, 1805, 1850*, ed. Wordsworth, Abams and Gill. The text quoted is that of the 1805 version.
4 Christopher Wordsworth, Jr to Joshua Watson, 14 June 1850; quoted in *The Prelude 1799, 1805. 1850*, p.539. See pp.529–40 for an account of how this description came into being, initiating from Wordsworth himself.
5 Northrop Frye, *Fearful Symmetry*, p.404.
6 Coleridge, *Selected Letters*, ed. H.J. Jackson, p.58.
7 Tzvetan Todorov, *The Fantastic*, p.8.
8 Mary Jacobus, 'Genre, Gender, and Autobiography: Vaudracour and Julia', in *Romanticism, Writing, and Sexual Difference*, p.202.
9 Harold Bloom, *The Anxiety of Influence*, p.5.
10 Bloom, *Anxiety*, pp.7–8.
11 Bloom, *Anxiety*, p.5.
12 Peter de Bolla, *Harold Bloom*, p.20.
13 Sandra M. Gilbert and Susan Gubar, *The Madwoman in the Attic*, p.47. For another feminist engagement with Bloom's ideas, see Annette Kolodny, 'A Map for Reading: Gender and the Interpretation of Literary Texts'.
14 Gilbert and Gubar, *Madwoman*, p.47.
15 For another attempt to replace Bloom's oedipal model of poetic influence with an alternative model which is also derived from psychoanaly-

sis, see Robin Jarvis, *Wordsworth, Milton and the Theory of Poetic Relations*, especially the first three chapters.

16 Sigmund Freud, 'On Narcissism: An Introduction' (1914), p.45.
17 Freud, 'On Narcissism', pp.32–3.
18 Wordsworth, 'Preface to *Lyrical Ballads*' (1802); quoted from Stephen Gill (ed.), *William Wordsworth*, pp.611–12.
19 Freud, 'On Narcissism', p.47.
20 Freud, 'On Narcissism', p.51.
21 Freud, 'On Narcissism', p.57.
22 Julia Kristeva, 'Freud and Love: Treatment and Its Discontents', in *The Kristeva Reader*, p.241.
23 Kristeva, 'Freud and Love', p.251.
24 Kristeva, 'Freud and Love', p.243.
25 Kristeva, 'Freud and Love', p.243.
26 Kristeva, 'Freud and Love', p.244.
27 Kristeva, 'Freud and Love', p.247.
28 Kristeva, 'Freud and Love', p.242.
29 Kristeva, 'Freud and Love', p.241.
30 Kristeva, 'Freud and Love', p.247.
31 Quoted from *Shelley's Poetry and Prose*, ed. Reiman and Powers.
32 Kristeva, 'Freud and Love', p.242.
33 Kristeva, 'Freud and Love', p.251.
34 Margaret Homans, *Women Writers and Poetic Identity*, p.37.
35 Tilottama Rajan, 'The Erasure of Narrative in Post-Structuralist Representations of Wordsworth'.
36 Tilottama Rajan, 'Romanticism and the Death of Lyric Consciousness', p.196.
37 Rajan, 'Romanticism', p.199.
38 Rajan, 'Romanticism', p.200.
39 Kristeva, 'Freud and Love', p.261.
40 Kristeva, 'Freud and Love', p.261.

# 4
## John Keats
### Effeminacy, drama
### and the performance of gender

Recent studies of John Keats's life and work have described a number of different ways in which his acts of self-presentation can be categorised as 'feminine' or reveal an often self-conscious adoption or appropriation of a feminine subject position.[1] A tendency to define the poet and his poetry in such terms can be traced back to early critical and vindictive reviews of his work which attempted to establish connections between the hierarchies of class and those of gender.[2] The most infamous of these contemporary reviews was, of course, that written by John Gibson Lockhart for the *Blackwood's Edinburgh Magazine* of August 1818, a review which stresses at its very outset a perceived relationship between gender and social status:

Of all the manias of this mad age, the most incurable, as well as the most common, seems to be no other than the *Metromanie*. The just celebrity of Robert Burns and Miss Baillie has had the melancholy effect of turning the heads of we know not how many farm-servants and unmarried ladies; our very footmen compose tragedies, and there is scarcely a superannuated governess in the island that does not leave a scroll of lyrics behind her in her band-box.[3]

Lockhart here attacks Keats's middle-class presumption, registered by his desire to be allowed access to the privileged world of the classically educated 'poet', by drawing analogies with servants and women and, from the perspective of gender criticism, it is significant that he exhibits no qualms about grouping lower-class 'farm-servants' with 'unmarried ladies' (of any class): for his purposes both are to be excluded from the realms of poetry. It is also worth noting that, in the second half of the quotation, Lockhart maps a generic distinction on to gender boundaries: the footmen aspire to the composition of 'tragedies' whereas the 'superannuated governess' is presumed only to practise the art of more lowly lyric poetry. Interestingly and revealingly, Lockhart initially establishes an equivalence between class and gender difference (upper/lower : male/female) and then, via genre classifications, reestablishes the existence of gender difference within a specific social class.

Nevertheless, in terms of the political significance of Keats's gendered subject position, one can see that the 'feminine' is at least at some level being associated with the politically and socially marginalised.[4] As Margaret Homans observes: 'if gender is a social construct, and if to be socially powerless is to be "a woman", then Keats can be classed among women.'[5] However, the conditionals here employed by Homans register dissatisfaction with an attempt at such clear-cut classification, and it is indeed too simple to conflate categories of class and gender in this way – even Lockhart's polemical critique of Keats's work reveals more complex internal tensions and ambiguities, as has been seen. Moreover, Keats's adoption of a 'feminine' subject position was not alluded to only by unsympathetic critics of his work: radical sympathisers such as William Hazlitt and Leigh Hunt also make it a central strand of their assessments of his achievement. In *Lord Byron and Some of His Contemporaries*, which was published in 1828, Leigh Hunt noted that 'Mr Keats's natural tendency to pleasure, as a poet, sometimes degenerated, by reason of his ill health, into a poetical effeminacy ... But Mr Keats was aware of this contradiction to the real energy of his nature, and prepared to get rid of it.'[6] Without reference to Keats's class position, Hunt too situates Keats's poetic practice within the domain of the 'feminine' or 'effeminate' and, like Lockhart, he sees such 'effeminacy' as a weakness and as something that the more 'manly' energy of the poet's true nature was constantly fighting against and attempting to master. Like Lockhart, but without the inflections of a class-related discourse, Hunt establishes an antithesis between successful poetic production and the 'feminine'. More famously, Hazlitt in his essay 'On Effeminacy of Character' described the apparent failings of Keats's poetry in very similar terms: 'I cannot help thinking that the fault of Mr Keats's poems was a deficiency in masculine energy of style. He had beauty, tenderness, delicacy, in an uncommon degree, but there was a want of strength and substance ... All is soft and fleshy, without bone and muscle.'[7] More will be said later in this chapter about Hazlitt's concept of (poetical) 'effeminacy' but, for the present, it should be noted that both Hazlitt and Hunt perceive central flaws in Keats's poetry which could be charted in terms of a standard opposition between, on the one hand, 'feminine' weaknesses related to delicacy, superficiality and sensual over-indulgence and, on the other, more 'masculine' virtues which they associate with strength, intellectual depth and self-restraint.

What is ironic about these criticisms is the fact that the grounds of complaint are remarkably similar to the premisses upon which Keats builds the foundations of his poetic programme: if Keats's poetry is 'effeminate' then the pronouncements made in his letters concerning his poetic beliefs would lead one to the conclusion that such effeminacy was for the poet the central strength rather than weakness of his poetic undertakings. In considering this adoption of 'effeminacy' as a poetic manifesto the most pertinent statement made by Keats is that which relates to his well-known concept of 'Negative Capability'. In a letter to George and Tom Keats written in the December of 1817, Keats describes the ideas that came to him following a wide-ranging discussion with his friend Charles Dilke:

at once it struck me, what quality went to form a Man of Achievement especially in Literature & which Shakespeare possessed so enormously – I mean *Negative Capability*, that is when man is capable of being in uncertainties, Mysteries, doubts, without any irritable reaching after fact & reason ... This pursued through Volumes would perhaps take us no further than this, that with a great poet the sense of Beauty overcomes every other consideration, or rather obliterates all consideration.[8]

Against rational certainty Keats places irrational uncertainty, against action he places passivity, against moral or social considerations he places the demands of 'Beauty': in all of these oppositions Keats rejects the ostensibly 'masculine' in favour of the apparently 'feminine' – his successful 'Man of Achievement' is, ironically, a man who has seemingly achieved a considerable degree of feminisation. As Anne Mellor comments: 'Keats' poetic theory is self-consciously positioned within the realm of the feminine gender ... A self that continually overflows itself, that melts into the Other, that *becomes* the Other, is conventionally associated with the female.'[9] This statement none the less contains its own tensions which reflect back on to ambiguities within Keats's own poetic project. If his poetic theory is one which is 'self-conscious' then such foregrounding of the 'self' and its intentions is surely at odds with the desire to lose the self in communion with the 'Other'. In a later letter Keats writes that:

A Poet is the most unpoetical of any thing in existence; because he has
no Identity – he is continually in for – and filling some other Body – The
Sun, the Moon, the Sea and Men and Women who are creatures of
impulse are poetical and have about them an unchangeable attribute –
the poet has none; no identity – he is certainly the most unpoetical of all
God's Creatures.[10]

The 'poet' has no 'identity' other than the identity he possesses as a
'poet': the logic here is circular, for the very attempt to define a poetic
identity highlights the paradoxical nature of the poet's position – he
is singled out for attention as a 'Man of Achievement' whilst simultaneously being denied a subject position from which to speak. The
ironies – and absurdities – of such a mode of argument are made
apparent as Keats continues in the letter: 'It is a wretched thing to
confess; but it is a very fact that not one word I ever utter can be
taken for granted as an opinion growing out of my identical nature
– how can it, when I have no nature?'[11] This is, of course, a joke but
it underlines the effective *impasse* that Keats has written himself into:
if the poet has no identity then he is excluded from the possibility of
meaningful communication and social interaction and, therefore, has
to forsake his claims to any significant cultural role. Denied a subject
position from which to speak, the poet has no voice other than that
borrowed from the discourse of others. Since he is a 'poet', Keats
seemingly claims, even the views expressed in the present letter lose
their authenticity.

Such problems, and the relationship between them and the question of Keats's (self-conscious) 'effeminacy', are brought into focus
by his 'Ode on Indolence'. In a journal-letter entry dated 19 March
1819, Keats records the feelings which were to give rise to the Ode:

This morning I am in a sort of temper indolent and supremely careless:
I long after a stanza or two of Thompson's Castle of indolence – My passions are all alseep [*for* asleep] from my having slumbered till nearly
eleven ... In this state of effeminacy the fibres of the brain are relaxed in
common with the rest of the body, and to such a happy degree that pleasure has no show of enticement and pain no unbearable frown. Neither
poetry, nor Ambition, nor Love have any alertness of countenance as
they pass by me: they seem rather like figures on a greek vase – a Man
and two women – whom no one but myself could distinguish in their
disguisement. This is the only happiness; and a rare instance of advantage in the body overpowering the Mind.[12]

In this passage Keats establishes all the expected oppositions between 'masculine' and 'feminine' qualities: the 'mind' has been subdued by the 'body', action is forsaken for inactivity, the social imperatives signalled by the appearance of 'Ambition' are rejected in favour of individual comfort. More interestingly, and problematically, Keats delineates this state of 'effeminacy' in opposition to two female figures, those of 'Love' and 'Poetry'. The nature of this opposition might initially appear confusing but it is a confusion which can be resolved through a consideration of the function being performed by the figure of 'Love'. As a seductive female presence, Love acts in a manner which is designed to tempt the 'effeminate' Keats into 'masculine' energy and virility – whilst 'Love' is personified as female, then, for Keats to succumb to the demands of love would be for him to act in a 'masculine' fashion. If we now turn from this to consider the role of 'poetry' in the passage, we begin to move towards a useful insight into the erotic dynamics of Keats's poetic theory, dynamics which problematise the assumed 'femininity' of his claims to 'Negative Capability'. 'Poetry', like 'Love', is personified as a seductive female: for Keats to pursue this feminine muse would be for him to arouse himself from his state of 'effeminacy' and adopt a more active, and thus 'masculine', subject position. Like Hazlitt and Hunt, therefore, Keats here asserts a fundamental opposition between poetry and effeminacy.

The tensions revealed through an analysis of this passage in the journal-letter become more marked when one turns to a consideration of the poem which emerges from it. Keats apparently writes a poem in praise of a state which excludes the possibility of poetic composition, a poem which, like the earlier letter about the paradoxical nature of the poet's 'identity', seems to undermine the basis of its own significance and authenticity:

> One morn before me were three figures seen,
>     With bowed necks, and joined hands, side-faced;
> And one behind the other stepped serene,
>     In placid sandals, and in white robes graced;
> They passed, like figures on a marble urn,
>     When shifted round to see the other side;
>         They came again; as when the urn once more
> Is shifted round, the first seen shades return;
>     And they were strange to me, as may betide
>         With vases, to one deep in Phidian lore. (1–10)[13]

The poem rehearses the situation described in the letter but, as a poem, this rehearsal contributes new difficulties, difficulties which are revealed initially through Keats's development of the simile of the 'marble urn'. The three figures represented here – Love, Ambition and Poetry – are portrayed as presenting themselves to the poet who presents himself as being in a similar state of languor or effeminacy to that described in the letter-journal. On closer examination, however, there is a blurring between the active and passive agents within this stanza. At one level it is the poet who is the passive spectator, at another, through the image of the vase being turned round to give the appearance of movement, it is presumably the poet–spectator who is initiating the action in order to create the illusion of action in the figures. The simile suggests that the autonomy of the figures is an illusion created by the poet and this illusion mirrors the corresponding illusion of the poet's apparent inaction at the moment of his active creation of the poem. The concluding lines of the stanza reveal an analogous ambiguity when the poet presents himself as one who is 'deep in Phidian lore', that is, one who has studied the work of Phidias, the sculptor of the Elgin Marbles. If this is the case, why should the figures on the vase appear 'strange'? Keats presents himself here as one who is both ignorant and knowledgeable at the same time, as someone who is privy to the secrets of an art similar to that of poetry and yet who is also an innocent or ignorant outsider. His ability to register the 'strange' quality of the figures would align him with the poet as defined in relation to 'Negative Capability': as someone who 'is capable of being in uncertainties, Mysteries, doubts, without any irritable reaching after fact & reason'. The deep study of 'Phidian lore', on the other hand, suggests a very different type of character and the repeated questioning of the figures in the remainder of the poem suggests that one aspect of the poet-figure presented here does indeed possess a desire to reach after 'fact' and is ultimately dissatisfied with a state composed solely of 'uncertainties'.

Helen Vendler describes the 'Ode on Indolence' in terms of the relationship between ontology and art:

Keats searches in *Indolence* for a proper mode of self-cognition. The speaking 'I' wishes, for the moment, to know itself solely as a being still in gestation, one whose senses have been laid to sleep and whose soul is an indolent lawn full of restless glimmers, dreamy budding, warmth, and overheard song. It does not wish to know itself in its erotic role as lover, its social role as seeker for fame, or its creative role as poet. It arduously repudiates the possibility that it may incarnate itself as an artifact.[14]

The irony here, of course, is that in writing a poem about this state of being, Keats inevitably does 'incarnate' his sense of 'self' in the form of an 'artifact' and this process of active artistic incarnation removes Keats's self-presentation from the 'feminine' to the 'masculine': Vendler's description of Keats's 'arduous' defence of the state of 'indolence' highlights such irony. Whilst apparently rejecting the lures of his female muse he has succumbed to them or, rather, whilst apparently subscribing to feminine self-effacement he has engaged in masculine self-assertion. In the final stanza of the poem these tensions become even more explicit when the poet asserts his desire for what he terms in the letter-journal 'effeminacy' by rejecting the apparently 'effeminate':

> So, ye three Ghosts, adieu! Ye cannot raise
>   My head cool-bedded in the flowery grass;
> For I would not be dieted with praise,
>   A pet-lamb in a sentimental farce!
> Fade softly from my eyes, and be once more
>   In masque-like figures on the dreamy urn.
>     Farewell! I yet have visions for the night,
> And for the day faint visions there is store.
>     Vanish, ye Phantoms, from my idle sprite
> Into the clouds, and never more return! (51–60)

Keats here turns away poetry and ambition because they would lead him to what he perceives to be a negatively 'feminine' position, that of a 'pet-lamb in a sentimental farce': the gendering of the poet's subject position becomes complex and ultimately confused and confusing. Anne Mellor concludes that 'The poem ends in an aporia, a void … Keats has separated himself from virile masculine action and from feminine productions, leaving him simultaneously without a gender identity and without a subject.'[15] 'Indolence' becomes meaningless when it is defended by self-assertion; self-assertion is negated when it has to rely upon passivity.

Whilst Mellor is right to suggest that this 'aporia' is what constitutes the conclusion of the Ode, her further comments upon the generic significances of such a conclusion are more questionable. She asserts that Keats's gender *impasse* is crucially involved with confused generic aspirations and claims that he was unable to write

those genres of poetic production that he himself defined as masculine: the Miltonic epic, the classical tragedy, the Shakespearean comedy. He remained attracted to those genres and subjects associated by his contemporaries with women: the ode and the romance; the affections, nature and art.[16]

The connections between gender and genre here are, I would argue, too crudely enforced. It is no doubt correct to see the productions of Shakespeare and Milton as being perceived as more 'manly' during this period (although, as will be seen later in this chapter, Keats and Hazlitt frequently gendered Shakespeare's abilities as implicitly 'feminine'). More problematic is the notion that Keats's 'contemporaries' (note the interesting shift in Mellor's argument from Keats's views to those of his contemporaries) would have thought of the 'ode and romance' as necessarily 'feminine'. Many women certainly did write poems in these genres – and were also dissuaded from writing more 'masculine' heroic tragedies and epics (see Lockhart's gender and genre distinctions observed earlier in his attack upon Keats) – but to claim that these genres were primarily associated 'with women' is conveniently to forget about, for example, the romances of Sir Walter Scott and the odes of William Wordsworth; and to suggest that tragedy was a genre reserved for male writers is to fail to pay attention to the large number of such plays written by Joanna Baillie and other extremely popular female playwrights of the period.[17]

There is a further specific difficulty in Mellor's claim that Keats was unable to write a 'classical tragedy': it is not clear what exactly is meant by 'classical' tragedy here but what is clear is that Keats was perfectly capable of composing a 'tragedy' – *Otho the Great* – which, although it has often been unfairly neglected by recent critics, was a play for which Keats entertained high hopes. It is also a work which implicitly and explicitly, both in its subject matter and its generic form, furthers an understanding of the troubled relationships between gender and genre in Keats's poetic practice. However, before turning to a consideration of the play itself, it is helpful to explore Keats's theories concerning acting and performance and how they relate to his poetic theories of 'Negative Capability' and, furthermore, how both of these relate to the performance of a gendered 'self'.

## II

It has long been recognised that an important element in the formation of Keats's notions of 'Negative Capability' was the poet's

appreciation and understanding of the acting style and abilities of
Edmund Kean.[18] Keats was an enthusiastic admirer of the actor and
wrote a sympathetic review of his performance in *Richard III* for *The
Champion* in 1817 in which he describes Kean's distinguishing tal-
ents in terms which bear a noticeable resemblance to those used to
depict the poet's own theories of poetic creation: 'Other actors are
continually thinking of their sum-total effect throughout a play. Kean
delivers himself up to the instant feeling, without the shadow of a
thought about anything else.'[19] Kean during performance is in a situation that is clearly analogous to that of the poet during the
moment of imaginative creation; in both there is a refusal to reach
after 'fact' and 'reason' whilst giving themselves up to the 'uncertainties' of the 'instant'. As the work of Jonathan Bate has shown, this
link between actor (as represented by Kean) and poet is an insight
that Keats largely owed to the dramatic criticism of William
Hazlitt.[20] For Hazlitt, another great admirer of Kean's work, the
actor should ideally lose himself in the role he is playing. In his essay
'On the Living Poets' he implicitly draws a parallel between the work
of poet and performer in relation to this:

Do you imagine that Shakespeare, when he wrote Lear or Othello, was
thinking of anything but Lear and Othello? Or that Mr. Kean, when he
plays these characters, is thinking of the audience? – No: he who would
be great in the eyes of others, must first learn to be nothing in his own.[21]

Like the poet according to Keats, the actor according to Hazlitt has
no 'identity' of his own; the fact that the actor and the poet must
both learn to be 'nothing' in order to achieve greatness resembles the
paradox of Keats's assertion of the necessary self-effacement and
effective 'feminisation' of the 'Man of Achievement' (as also represented by Shakespeare) in his letter quoted in the last section.

However, the resemblance to the paradox contained within Keats's
letter would suggest that Hazlitt's presentation of Kean's acting abilities is not without its own inner tensions and, on further analysis,
this indeed turns out to be the case. Whilst implicitly suggesting that
Kean has the ability to lose his own 'self' within the part he is playing, Hazlitt also wishes to define the actor as someone who has an
immediately recognisable artistic identity: 'Mr. Kean's manner of
acting this part has one particular advantage; it is entirely his own,
without any traces of imitation of any other actor. He stands upon
his own ground, and he stands firm upon it. Almost every scene has

the stamp and freshness of nature.'[22] Hazlitt presents us with another paradox here: whilst appreciating the character being performed (and not apparently thinking of the actor playing the part), the spectator is also simultaneously aware of the specific performance and the particular abilities of the individual actor who is using the occasion to reveal his claims to theatrical greatness. Even Hazlitt's choice of metaphor at the end of the quotation suggests an implicit tension – 'nature' is not inherent in the performance (how could it be when the play is by its very nature a fabrication?) but something which is 'stamped' on to it and therefore, ironically, 'unnatural'.

Although Hazlitt does not express the concerns of his arguments in such terms, it can be seen that the tensions between identity and self-effacement, and between art and nature are those which in Keats's theoretical pronouncements are clearly gendered. Indeed, elsewhere in Hazlitt's critical writings one can see the troublesome inconsistencies in his theories revealing themselves in terms of gender. In an essay on 'The Indian Jugglers' he again takes up the notion of 'greatness' in relation to acting:

No act terminating in itself constitutes greatness. This will apply to all displays of power or trials of skill, which are confined to the momentary, individual effort, and construct no permanent image or trophy of themselves without them. Is not an actor then a great man, because 'he dies and leaves the world no copy?' I must make an exception for Mrs. Siddons, or else give up my definition of greatness for her sake.[23]

The problem remains unresolved but, interestingly, the actor's self-terminating act is related to a lack of masculine virility – he is unable to establish a patrilineal line. (One is reminded by this barren 'act terminating in itself' of Byron's opinion that Keats's poetry was a 'sort of mental masturbation').[24] In another essay from *Table-talk*, 'On Effeminacy of Character', Hazlitt writes of the vices of those who suffer from 'effeminacy' in terms which suggest the ideal virtues of the actor, particularly as they are presented by Keats in his *Champion* piece quoted earlier: 'They live in the present moment, are the creatures of the present impulse (whatever it may be) – and beyond that, the universe is nothing to them.'[25] The actor whose skill for Keats lies in being able to deliver 'himself up to the instant feeling, without the shadow of a thought for anything else' would, from this evidence, be 'effeminate' in Hazlitt's terms.

However, as has been suggested, it is not the case that Keats and

Hazlitt fundamentally disagree about either acting or poetry: it would be fairer to say that they are both attempting to voice similar aesthetic theories and struggling with similar ambiguities and contradictions as a result. Hazlitt's fear is that the 'effeminate' is somehow both unproductive and irresponsible: he praises Kean's ability to lose a sense of 'self' and yet at the same time wishes to establish the actor's 'identity' in order to provide his art with a more permanent worth, something that will transcend the limitations of the 'present impulse'. One way in which he attempts to do this in his theatrical criticism is in his repeated tendency to relate Kean's 'art' to a more permanent artistic practice – that of painting. This is evident, for example, in his comments on Kean's *Richard III* which were cited earlier: 'Mr. Kean's attitude in leaning against the side of the stage before he comes forward in this scene, was one of the most graceful and striking we remember to have seen. It would have done for Titian to paint.'[26] It is again to be found in a later review of the same role: 'Mr. Kean's acting in Richard, as we before remarked in his Shylock, presents a perpetual succession of striking pictures. He bids fair to supply us with the best Shakespear [*sic*] Gallery we have had!'[27] In the discussion of Keats's 'Ode on Indolence' I suggested that there was in that poem (and in Keats's poetic theory) a tension between the indolent/effeminate state that Keats was advocating and the actual production of a poetic artefact that would allow the poet to communicate meaningfully from an established subject position. There is a similar tension being enacted in the analogies that Hazlitt makes between Kean and the art of the painter. In order for Kean's work to achieve a permanent status, in order for it to communicate the greatness of the actor as artist, it must be seen to leave a more permanent legacy than simply the ephemeral memory of an enacted role in which the 'identity' of the actor was erased. Hazlitt's analogy with painting denies the dramatic flux of theatre but intimates that drama aspires to the condition of a more permanent – and therefore more elevated – art form.[28]

In this assertion of permanence and fixity over the ephemeral and uncertain, Hazlitt is implicitly making a claim for the 'masculine' over the 'feminine' and attempting to 'masculinise' an art which, according to his very own aesthetic definitions, is in danger of being viewed as dangerously 'feminine'. In making the analogy with pictorial art, Hazlitt constructs a metaphorical 'frame' around Kean's stage performance and allows it to be viewed according to different – and more traditionally respectable – aesthetic criteria. This act of 'framing' can be usefully seen in terms of Robert Young's account of Jacques Derrida's notion of the 'parergon':

The parergon, a word that Derrida finds in Kant, is the supplement to the 'ergon' (work) – against, beside, above and beyond it. In the visual arts, the parergon will be the frame, or drapery, or enclosing column. The parergon could also be a (critical) text, which 'encloses' another text. But what it precisely is not, is a simple inside/outside dichotomy.[29]

Hazlitt's drama criticism is ostensibly 'outside' the actual dramatic performance provided by Kean but, because it provides the actor with an apparent artistic aspiration, it alters the nature of the 'inside' and requires a different kind of response on the part of the spectator. No longer allowing themselves to be carried along by the passions and 'impulses' of the moment, the audience will search for the more lasting aesthetic satisfactions intimated by Hazlitt's criticism. In this way, the critic's apparently external comments (the 'parergon') become a crucial aspect of the work they refer to (the 'ergon'). Indeed, Hazlitt's prose effectively provides the 'permanent' (because written) complement to Kean's ephemeral performance. To put this in alternative, gendered, terms, Hazlitt provides the gloss of a 'masculinist' aesthetic to the 'feminine' uncertainties of the actor's art.

In his discussion of Derrida, Young also notes that 'framing must always occur in both senses – pictorial and criminal' by which he means that the act of 'framing' must also be one of misrepresentation or misreading: the critical text reproduces the 'original' in light of its own interpretative strategies.[30] This legal metaphor is interesting, but another way of reading the 'framing' practised in Hazlitt's reading of Kean would be to see the critic as a judge applying aesthetic 'laws' to the actor's performance; the critic polices the dramatic act and ensures that it respects the demands of the preceding written text. Hazlitt himself makes use of such an analogy:

Those who put themselves upon their trial, must, however, submit to the verdict; and the critic in general does little more than prevent a lingering death, by anticipating, or putting in immediate force, the sentence of the public. The victims of criticism, like the victims of the law, bear no good will to their executioners; and I confess I have often been heartily tired of so thankless an office. What I have said of any actor, has never arisen from private pique of any sort.[31]

The actor's lack of 'identity' is countered by the critic's alleged public impersonality: the critic applies the apparently fixed laws of artistic taste to control the possible excesses of dramatic performance.

In this section I have suggested that there are clear links between Keats's theories of 'Negative Capability' and his theories of dramatic performance (which can be closely linked to the influential ideas of William Hazlitt). Both poetic and dramatic theories are evidently gendered as both actor and poet are perceived as being 'effeminate' in their ability to efface their own identities during artistic activity. Having said this, for both Hazlitt and Keats this 'effeminacy' is a cause for some misgiving, and both writers attempt in various ways to introduce a more 'masculine' role for the artist which relies upon a greater sense of self-assertion and artistic awareness. If, as was suggested at the beginning of this chapter in the discussion of Lockhart's review article, the 'effeminate' was to a certain extent seen as disruptive or subversive, then the re-assertion of the 'masculine' represents a return to more socially acceptable artistic practice – hence Hazlitt's use of the legal metaphor in relation to his dramatic criticism. This tension between 'masculine' and 'feminine' artistic practice – and between the socially acceptable and the socially subversive – emerges interestingly in a letter to Benjamin Bailey that Keats wrote in 1819 where, significantly for the present argument, he is describing his progress in the composition of *Otho the Great*. Keats tells Bailey that he has

completed 4 Acts of a Tragedy. It was the opinion of most of my friends that I should never be able to write a scene – I will endeavour to wipe away the prejudice – I sincerely hope you will be pleased when my Labours since we last saw each other shall reach you – One of my Ambitions is to make as great a revolution in modern dramatic writing as Kean has done in acting – another to upset the drawling of the blue stocking literary world.[32]

In this letter Keats asserts his right to inclusion into the realm of successful poets through his achievement in the writing of a successful tragedy but, ironically, he presents this claim to canonical status in terms of 'revolution' and effective subversion of the literary establishment. He typifies the 'literary world' as effeminate blue-stockings, and postures as the writer of more 'manly' tragedies, and yet aligns himself with Kean's artistic practice which, like his own poetic endeavours, has been seen to be gendered as 'feminine'. The tensions revealed in this letter highlight Keats's own uncertainties about

issues of poetry and gender and the relationship of both to the possibilities of effective social intervention by the artist.[33] Furthermore,
the fact that Keats is here writing about the composition of a play
introduces more explicitly the question of genre: if Keats's understanding of Kean's acting abilities crucially impinges upon the development of his ideas about poetics and gender, how are both of these
concerns revealed in a play, *Otho the Great*, which Keats wrote with
the intention that Kean himself should perform the leading role?[34]

### III

The process of *Otho the Great*'s composition was an unusual one, as
the play was in many ways a joint undertaking between Keats and his
friend Charles Brown. In his *Life of John Keats*, Brown provides a
detailed account of how the work came to be written:

> I engaged to furnish him with the fable, characters, and dramatic con-
> duct of a tragedy, and he was to embody it into poetry. The progress of
> this work was curious; for, while I sat opposite to him, he caught my
> description of each scene, entered into the characters to be brought for-
> ward, the events, and every thing connected with it. Thus he went on,
> scene after scene, never knowing nor enquiring into the scene which was
> to follow until four acts were completed. It was then he required to
> know, at once, all the events which were to occupy the fifth act. I
> explained them to him; but, after a patient hearing, and some thought,
> he insisted on it that my incidents were too numerous, and, as he termed
> them, too melodramatic. He wrote the fifth act in accordance with his
> own view.[35]

The first thing to be noticed here is how Brown's account recalls
Keats's description of the ideal state of both the poet and the actor.
As he wrote the play Keats was in a state which consisted of 'doubts'
and 'uncertainties' as to the outcome of the narrative; like Kean in
*Richard III*, the poet had to deliver 'himself up to the instant feeling,
without the shadow of a thought about anything else'. Like the poet
in a state of 'Negative Capability', Keats as he wrote *Otho the Great*
attempted to exist in a condition which precluded any 'irritable
reaching' after information which related to anything beyond the
present moment. As poet he effectively 'acted out' the emotions of
the characters he was creating and, as in the case of the actor, this
acting out involved an 'effeminate' denial of the 'self'.

However, as Brown records it, this state of 'Negative Capability' ceased to exist before the play had been completed. Upon reaching the fifth act (the point gained when he wrote the letter to Bailey quoted earlier in which he declares his 'masculine' ambitions as a poet), Keats declares a desire to move from the state of uncertainty to one of knowledge, a move which signals a parallel desire for 'Negative Capability' to be replaced by artistic self-awareness. In his criticisms of Brown's programme for the play's completion, Keats exhibits an understanding of what is required to transform arbitrary narrative events into the artistic form of heroic tragedy. The fact that he rejects Brown's proposals as too 'melodramatic' is significant, but it is a significance which can easily be missed. Aileen Ward, for example, notes that:

It is hard to imagine how Brown's ending could have been more melodramatic than the one Keats actually wrote; it is still harder to understand why Keats apparently found greater satisfaction in writing the last act of *Otho* than in composing any of his other poems.[36]

The final events of *Otho the Great* might be 'melodramatic' according to current usage of the word but it is probable that Keats meant something quite different from Ward's meaning when he used the word. An article in an edition of *New British Theatre* from 1814, which is quoted by the *Oxford English Dictionary* as an example for one of its definitions of the word, makes a useful distinction between the conclusions of melodramas and those of tragedy and comedy: 'In tragedy and comedy the final event is the effect of the moral operations of the different characters, but in the melo-drama the catastrophe is the physical result of mechanical strategem.'[37] The suggestion here is that the 'higher' dramatic forms, such as tragedy, depend ultimately upon a more permanent set of 'moral' values and laws to which the characters and their actions relate whereas 'lower' forms, such as the melodrama, are solely dependent upon the external and arbitrary forces represented by physical action on the stage. Keats's desire to avoid the 'melodramatic', therefore, can be seen as a continuation of his desire to move from the position of 'actor' (necessarily caught up only in the immediate physicality of stage performance) to that of self-conscious artist (who can perceive things according to their larger, more permanent significances). It is, in effect, a rejection of the 'body' in favour of the 'mind' and, by implication, a rejection of the 'feminine' in favour of the 'masculine': one recalls that state of 'effeminacy' which formed the starting point for

the 'Ode on Indolence', a state which Keats described as 'a rare
instance of advantage in the body overpowering the Mind'. In the
final act of *Otho the Great* Keats wished to reassert the mind's power
over the body and thus reject such 'effeminacy'.

Throughout the play, however, one can detect an interest in the
complex relationships that exist between 'mind' and 'body', or, to put
this another way, in the tensions that inevitably develop due to the
gap between notions of inner 'truth' and an individual's 'performance' of the self. The play is crucially concerned with images and
instances of disguise and deception and with the abilities and inabil-
ities of the spectator to distinguish between truth and falsehood. In
the first act, for instance, Otho acts with apparent generosity to the
defeated Gersa, the Prince of Hungary, and, in a telling speech, he
attempts to convince Gersa, as well as those around him, of the
essential sincerity of his actions:

> Though I did hold you high in my esteem
> For your self's sake, I do not personate
> The stage-play emperor to entrap applause,
> To set the silly sort o' the world agape,
> And make the politic smile; no, I have heard
> How in the Council you condemned this war,
> Urging the perfidy of broken faith –
> For that I am your friend. (I.ii.142–9)

This speech establishes a significant opposition between notions of
an individual 'self' and the performance of specific acts by an individual – and appears to value action above inner essence. Otho
claims to have regarded Gersa with 'esteem' due to the intrinsic qualities revealed by his essential 'self' but, notwithstanding this, his
friendship only develops through an awareness of Gersa's actions in
the 'Council' where he argued against the war in which he has now
been defeated. It might be the case, of course, that Gersa has acted
in the way he has because such action was dictated by the essential
characteristics of the self, implying that a person's actions are a way
(perhaps the only way) of knowing what they 'really' are and suggesting a perfect match between internal and external, mind and
body. The rest of the speech problematises the possibility of such a
perfect equivalence, however, through its introduction of the
imagery of dramatic performance and its ambiguous sentence construction. Is Otho personating a 'stage emperor' or not? Does his

speech register an admission of pretence of some kind or should it be read as a declaration of 'sincerity'? If Otho is revealing an act of deception then this reveals an ironic awareness of the performative nature of kingship but it also undercuts the possibility of any final notion of 'friendship' based upon mutual self-knowledge. Indeed, any conception of an essential 'self' is lost in the idea of 'performance' because the self itself becomes a role to be played. Otho's speech would seem to suggest, then, that the true 'self' can only be known through performance but also that, paradoxically, performance can be no guarantee of sincerity.

The surface meaning of Otho's speech, of course, is that he is acting out the role of 'emperor' as an emperor and that there is an essential connection between who he is and what he does that has no reliance upon anything or anyone else. In this he is claiming to act in a way similar to the poet or the actor as described by Hazlitt in a passage quoted earlier:

Do you imagine that Shakespeare, when he wrote Lear or Othello, was thinking of anything but Lear and Othello? Or that Mr. Kean, when he plays these characters, is thinking of his audience? – No: he who would be great in the eyes of others, must first learn to be nothing in his own.

Otho's claim to greatness as an emperor is that he is at one with his 'role' and has no need of an 'audience' to confirm his status. None the less, this is a public declaration and, as has been seen, the ambiguities implicit within the speech undermine the assumed sincerity it contains. Commenting upon Keats's depiction of Otho throughout the play, Daniel P. Watkins notes the 'discrepancies between apparent integrity and actual political motive' and reaches the conclusion that, as far as Otho is concerned, 'political expediency motivates his benevolence'.[38]

Watkins associates Otho's manipulation of performance with the exploitative nature of the patriarchal society in which he exerts his power: this is undoubtedly justified at one level but it is also the case that the uncertain blurring of distinction between action and essence highlights a fundamental insecurity within that very society. In her study of the roles played by women within the play, Catherine Burroughs notes the ways in which Auranthe, the sister of the scheming Conrad whom the hero, Ludolph, tragically loves and marries, 'skillfully impersonates a number of characters' and 'employs acting techniques to thwart societal repression'.[39] Burroughs's aim is to construct the performative nature of Auranthe's character as self-empowering by adopting the strategy of 'performing' her part against the grain of Keats's written text. Again, there is a certain credibility in this but it fails to convince entirely because of its failure to take into consideration the 'performative' nature of so many of the characters in the play as a whole – for example, the character of Otho himself as depicted by Watkins and in the earlier discussion here. What one can say, however, is that Auranthe's role-shifting represents, from a patriarchal perspective, a general uneasiness about the instabilities of 'self' that the performative nature of such a society is reliant upon. The society of the play (and that of early nineteenth-century England) requires the assertion of a strong 'masculine' self that is in control of the 'roles' it performs and yet, because the success of the 'self' is dependent upon the performances it provides, rather than upon its intrinsic nature, the very grounds for the 'self' are undermined. These are the same concerns and worries that underlie Keats's uncertainties about 'Negative Capability', a theory which also relies upon 'performance' and 'feminine' role-shifting but which again threatens the achievement of 'masculine' success and recognition. The changing nature of Auranthe in the play (wicked schemer or hapless victim of her brother's machinations?; sexually naive or rapacious?) reveals a fear of a situation where the 'self' is unknowable and, significantly, this fear is mapped on to a female character.

Ludolph's insanity in the final act is the result of his failure to reconcile the two conflicting images of Auranthe that co-exist within his mind: that of the innocent bride and that of the duplicitous sexual manipulator. The disintegration of his own sense of 'self' is precipitated by the collapse of his construction of her own 'identity'. Losing Auranthe in a forest in the final act, Ludolph indirectly reveals how the stability of his own self is threatened by his uncertainties about his bride:

> She's gone! – I cannot clutch her! No revenge!
> A muffled death, ensnared in horrid silence!
> Suckled to my grave amid a dreary calm!
> O, where is that illustrious noise of war,
> To smother up this sound of labouring breath,
> The rustle of the trees! (V.i.25–30)

It is uncertain at first whose 'muffled death' he is describing: that of

Auranthe lost in the wood or his own due to his despair at having
lost her (both literally and metaphorically). It soon becomes clear
that it is the latter to which he is referring but it is also clear that what
is being contemplated here is a version of death closely associated
with a fear of the 'feminine' and, specifically, the maternal. The 'feminine'/maternal leads to death of the self ('Suckled to my grave') and
can be countered only by an appeal to a more 'masculine' form of
heroic action ('where is that illustrious noise of war'). 'Labouring
breath' conjures up the image of a maternal bringing forth of death
although the fact that the breath (which would logically be that of
Ludolph himself) is presented as a metaphor for the 'rustle of the
trees' suggests also the ongoing dissolution of his sense of 'self': in
his state of emotional and ontological confusion, the boundaries
between external and internal are destroyed and the centre of
Ludolph's consciousness is dispersed. Ludolph's desire for 'revenge'
and the opportunity for martial valour reveal his fear of being
'[s]mothered' to death but they also intimate his need for a stable,
knowable self which guarantees its own validity through its performance. It is such a 'performance' that Ludolph, in his madness,
attempts to enact in the final scene of the play, a scene which, like
much of the rest of the play, possesses an ironically self-reflexive concern with issues of theatricality.

Plunged into madness by the revelation of Auranthe's deception,
Ludolph exists solely in a world created by his own deranged mind,
a world that the other characters in the play take care to respect. As
Ethelbert the Abbot advises in the penultimate scene:

> his very motions,
> Nods, becks and hints, should be obeyed with care,
> Even on the moment: so his troubled mind
> May cure itself. (V.iv.31–4)

As Ludolph acts out his madness his actions are thus observed in a
way similar to those of an actor on the stage – every movement and
gesture is carefully noted by the attentive court who effectively play
the part of a responsive audience in the theatre. However, it is also
the case, of course, that they too are 'acting' in that they are indulging
Ludolph's madness by obeying his requests and following his whims
as if he were behaving sanely. This final scene, therefore, enacts a
complicated relationship between 'performance' and the notion of
'reality': Ludolph, in a state of madness, believes in the 'reality' of the

part he is playing but is perceived by the others to be acting against his 'true' self; the court, on the other hand, whilst they maintain a grip on what they see as 'reality', perform a role which belies the 'truth' of Ludolph's madness.[40]

The cause of Ludolph's madness is, in effect, this very confusion between performance and reality as it is embodied in Auranthe; for the Prince, Auranthe's duplicitous femininity epitomises all of his fundamental ontological doubts: 'Her lips – I swear no human bones e'er wore / So taking a disguise' (V.v.69–70). Here the skin itself – the visible body – becomes a 'disguise' and thus Ludolph expresses an extreme rejection of the 'feminine', both literally in his dismissal of Auranthe as a woman and more broadly in his distrust of the physical and bodily. In place of such 'femininity' Ludolph desires to reassert a 'masculine' control and, in the literal action of the play, this desire manifests itself in his wish to kill his bride.[41] That this is a specifically 'masculine' self-assertion is made evident through the language of male sexual desire:

> the hour
> Draws near when I must make a winding up
> Of bridal mysteries. A fine-spun vengeance!
> Carve it on my tomb, when I rest beneath
> Men shall confess – This Prince was gulled and cheated,
> But from the ashes of disgrace he rose
> More than a fiery dragon, and did burn
> His ignominy up in purging fires! (V.v.127–34)

Throughout the final scene Ludolph's anticipation of the murder of Auranthe is figured in terms of sexual consummation: the 'bridal mysteries' will comprise the death of the bride at the hands of her husband.

However, if this anticipated act is intended as a reassertion of (a masculine) 'self', it is also one which is beset with its own inner contradictions. At the moment he looks forward to an act which will establish 'truth', Ludolph envisages it in terms of an act of representation; instead of the act itself the Prince thinks in terms of a written record of the act ('Carve it on my tomb') and of the act transformed into a narrative on the lips of others ('Men shall confess'). This is a prevalent tendency in the scene as a whole:

> Awake, awake!
> Put on a judge's brow, and use a tongue
> Made iron-stern by habit! Thou shalt see
> A deed to be applauded, 'scribed in gold! (V.v.144–7)

Ludolph comes to see the anticipated murder of his wife as a performance, a performance which requires a confirmation of validity
which can be provided only by others, as applause can be provided
only by an audience. Rather than a self-affirming, 'masculine' act,
therefore, the murder is in danger of slipping into an act merely performed for effect, one which falls short of the consummatory union
of mind and body, self and action. That this is the case is revealed in
the closing moments of the play where Ludolph believes he is carrying out the murder only to find that he has, in reality, merely been
hallucinating:

> There she is! Take that! And that! No, no –
> That's not well done. Where is she? (V.v.183–4)

Auranthe does in fact die but her death remains a mystery – all that
can be said is that its cause is unrelated to Ludolph's agency. The
Prince's acting out of the murder on stage is just that, a mere acting
out, and, as such, it can have no lasting effect. Like Kean's dramatic
performance, or Keats's poet in a state of 'Negative Capability',
Ludolph's presentation of his madness results in a denial rather than
an assertion of the self. The Prince dies and the curtain falls and the
audience is left with a sense of Ludolph's failure to control the 'feminine' excesses of both Auranthe and his own performance.

## IV

Ludolph in the final scene of *Otho the Great* can be said to be enact-
ing the paradox felt by the Keatsian poet. Desiring to produce a work
of lasting importance – 'A deed to be applauded' – the poet is none
the less dependent upon a creative strategy which has its foundations
in the notion of a performance where 'fact & reason' are discarded in
favour of a 'feminine' delight in 'doubts' and 'Mysteries'. 'Masculine'
certainty and fixity, which were implicitly seen by Keats as necessary
for the achieved work of art, are denied by the very artistic approach
adopted, just as Auranthe's murder is rendered impossible by the
mad performance that Ludolph believes will bring about her death.
Both Ludolph and the poet fail to control or fix that state of femi-

ninity (represented in the play by Auranthe) which both troubles them and, effectively, inspires them to act in the first place.

*Otho the Great*, whilst not belonging to the normal canon of Keats's most widely read and studied work, takes us to some of the major concerns of his poetry as a whole. In Ludolph's ambiguous relationship with Auranthe we see repeated other, more familiar, moments in Keats's poetry. One thinks, for example, of 'Ode to a Nightingale' in which the poet is drawn towards, and yet ultimately rejects, the song of a bird which is both femininely seductive and darkly destructive of the poet's sense of self:

> Darkling I listen; and, for many a time
>    I have been half in love with easeful Death,
> Called him soft names in many a mused rhyme,
>    To take into the air my quiet breath;
> Now more than ever seems it rich to die,
>    To cease upon the midnight with no pain,
>       While thou art pouring forth thy soul abroad
>          In such an ecstasy.
> Still would thou sing, and I have ears in vain -
>    To thy high requiem become a sod. (51–60)

The desire to mingle with the bird's song suggests the passivity and denial of self that Keats advocates in his discussion of 'Negative Capability', but this (feminine) self-denial, as we have seen, is problematic because it removes the poet's own (masculine) identity. If Keats succumbs to the lure of the bird's song then he metaphorically 'dies' as a poet, cut off from the very thing which provided his inspiration. In place of the bird's song, the reader is presented with Keats's own poem which controls a potentially threatening experience by recounting it in verse. Yet the narrative that the successful poem recounts is one of failure: although the bird has in one sense been captured by the poem, in another it has escaped the poet's control:

> Adieu! adieu! Thy plaintive anthem fades
>    Past the near meadows, over the still stream,
>       Up the hill-side; and now 'tis buried deep
>          In the next valley-glades:
> Was it a vision, or a waking dream?
>       Fled is that music ... Do I wake or sleep? (75–80)

The poem can be read both as a document of imaginative success and also as a record of imaginative failure. Just as Ludolph both kills and fails to kill Auranthe, so the persona of Keats in 'Ode to a Nightin-gale' both succeeds and fails as a poet. The confusion suggested by the dream-like endings of both texts ('Do I wake or sleep?') registers the similar ambiguity of their achievements.

Ludolph's performance in the final scene, then, is in fact a kind of non-performance in that it fails to achieve the ends it desires, and this failure, it has been suggested, can be related to larger issues within Keats's poetry as a whole. Marlon B. Ross notes that Keats's rejec-tion of 'masculine' modes of poetic discourse were to prove ulti-mately debilitating:

When he tries to explore nonpatrilineal uses of language, however, he is immediately perceived, and perceives himself, as impotent. To hesitate patrilineal performance is to refuse patriarchal power; to refuse patriar-chal power means to give up power as it is practised within culture; to have no power within culture makes it all the more difficult to have power over culture, to have power to change culture. How can one reject the signs of power and still be empowered?[42]

Keats's 'impotence' as Ross describes it here is Ludolph's 'impotence' in the final scene when he is unable to achieve the sexually conceived consummation of Auranthe's death. None the less, what *Otho the Great* also reveals is the fact that the 'performance' of 'patriarchal power' is always threatened by hesitancy and doubt, forever troubled by the resurgence of a feminine 'other' which refuses to be con-trolled. Keats's depiction of Ludolph might reveal his own insecuri-ties as a poet but those insecurities relate back to more widely held doubts within society as a whole. In choosing to write a tragedy, Keats was provided with the opportunity to explore the relationship between his own theories of poetry and his ideas of dramatic perfor-mance, both of which he thought of in gendered terms. The result-ing play dramatised the tensions inherent in both and also, as a result, provided an enactment of the instabilities of masculinity in the early nineteenth century.

### NOTES

1 My approach in the present chapter is indebted to a number of recent studies which investigate similar aspects of Keats's work. For example: Margaret Homans, 'Keats Reading Women, Women Reading Keats'; Anne K. Mellor, *Romanticism and Gender*, especially pp.171–86; Marlon B. Ross, *The Contours of Masculine Desire*, especially pp.155–86; Marlon

B. Ross, ' "Beyond the Fragmented Word": Keats at the Limits of Patrilineal Language'; Susan J. Wolfson, 'Feminizing Keats'; Nicholas Roe, 'Keats's Lisping Sedition'; Alan Bewell, 'Keats's Realm of Flora'; and, from a slightly different perspective, Marjorie Levinson, *Keats's Life of Allegory*, especially pp.1–44.

2 The most detailed account of attempts to place Keats's work within a 'feminised' framework is offered by Susan J. Wolfson in 'Feminizing Keats'.

3 From Theodore Redpath (ed.), *The Young Romantics and Critical Opinion*, p.467.

4 Nicholas Roe claims that 'the diction of Keats's poetry, glossed by the reviewers as an "effeminate" and childish lisp, articulated the subversive challenge of beauty to the discourse of the political and cultural establishment' ('Lisping Sedition', p.49).

5 Homans, 'Keats Reading Women', p.342.

6 Leigh Hunt, quoted in G.M. Matthews (ed.), *Keats: The Critical Heritage*, pp.251–2.

7 William Hazlitt, 'On Effeminacy of Character' from *Table-talk; or, Original Essays on Men and Manners* (1821–22, 1824); *Works*, VIII.254–5.

8 *Letters of John Keats*, ed. Gittings, p.43.

9 Anne K. Mellor, *Romanticism and Gender*, pp.174–5.

10 To Richard Woodhouse, 27 October 1818; *Letters*, p.157.

11 *Letters*, p.158.

12 To George and Georgina Keats, 14 February – 3 May 1819, *Letters*, p.228.

13 The edition of Keats's poems used thoughout is *The Poems of John Keats*, ed. Miriam Allott.

14 Helen Vendler, *The Odes of John Keats*, p.37.

15 Mellor, *Romanticism and Gender*, p.182.

16 Mellor, *Romanticism and Gender*, p.182.

17 Catherine Burroughs goes so far as to ascribe to Baillie a 'feminist theatre theory' in her 'personification of Tragedy as a wife or mother' and her use of the genre as one which relies upon the power of private and domestic emotion which remains hidden frrom the (masculine) public sphere ('Acting in the Closet', p.126).

18 See, for example, Robert Gittings, *John Keats*, pp.171–5, and Jonathan Bate, *Shakespeare and the English Romantic Imagination*, pp.165–74.

19 Keats, *The Champion*, 21 December 1817; quoted in Bate, *Shakespeare and the English Romantic Imagination*, p.166.

20 David Bromwich has discussed more general (as well as other specific) ways in which Keats was influenced by Hazlitt: 'What he found most useful were Hazlitt's doubts about the predominance of the self in modern poetry: the egotistical, Hazlitt taught, was only one version of the sublime, and a limited one' (*Hazlitt: The Mind of a Critic*, p.363).

21 William Hazlitt, 'On the Living Poets', *Lectures on the English Poets* (1818, 1819), in *Works*, V.145.

22 William Hazlitt, *A View of the English Stage; or, A Series of Dramatic Criticisms* (1818); in *Works*, V.180. Originally a review of Kean's *Richard III* from the *Morning Chronicle* of 15 February 1814.

23 William Hazlitt, 'The Indian Jugglers', *Table Talk*, in *Works*, VIII.85. It is interesting to compare Hazlitt's definition of what constitutes 'greatness' with Adam Smith's definition of 'unproductive labour' which 'produces nothing which afterwards would purchase or procure an equal quantity of labour': 'Like the declamation of the actor, the harangue of the orator, or the tune of the musician, the work of all of them perishes in the very instant of its production.' See Adam Smith, *An Enquiry into the Nature and Causes of the Wealth of Nations*, II.3. Sarah Siddons, who is cited by Hazlitt as an exception to his generalisations, presents problems which cannot be entered into fully here. Although Siddons is often seen to have provided a model for proper, if at times excessive, feminine sensibility (see, for example, Coral Anne Howells, *Love, Mystery, And Misery*, pp.9–10, and Jeffrey N. Cox (ed.), *Seven Gothic Dramas*, p.53), Hazlitt thought of her as offering a balancing of gendered attributes in that she 'united both extremes of acting, that is, all the frailties of passion, with all the strength and resources of the intellect' (*Works*, V.211). For a further discussion of Siddons in relation to Keats, see Catherine Burroughs, 'Acting in the Closet', pp.135–8; for a more general discussion of the ambiguities present in accounts of her acting, see Julie A. Carlson, *In the Theatre of Romanticism*, pp.162–8.
24 Byron, letter to John Murray, 9 September 1820, in *Byron's Letters and Journals*. ed Marchand, VIII.225. For discussions of Keats and masturbation see Mellor, *Romanticism and Gender*, pp.173–4; and Levinson, *Keats's Life of Allegory*, esp. pp.18–29. Nicholas Roe relates Byron's comments to issues of social class: 'Byron's social-sexual slander betrayed his own insecurities, his need to deny Keats's imaginative presence and reaffirm his own socio-poetic virility as a member of the aristocracy' ('Lisping Sedition', p.47).
25 Hazlitt, *Table-talk, Works*, VIII.248.
26 Hazlitt, *A View of the English Stage, Works*, V.182.
27 Hazlitt, *A View of the English Stage, Works*, V.184.
28 For another discussion of Hazlitt's use of imagery derived from the visual arts in his drama criticism, see Roy Park, *Hazlitt and the Spirit of the Age*, pp.138–58.
29 Robert Young (ed.), *Untying the Text*, p.226.
30 Young, *Untying the Text*, p.226.
31 Hazlitt, *A View of the English Stage, Works*, V.177.
32 To Benjamin Bailey, 14 August 1819; *Letters*, p. 276.
33 Alan Bewell has discussed these tensions in terms of Keats's use of floral imagery in his poetry: 'One effect of the antagonism expressed in the 1817 and 1818 reviews of Keats's poetry is that it split the poetry along gender lines. The fundamental unresolved conflict of Keats's later verse lies in this struggle ... to distance himself from the intimacy with women and women's floral style that he sought in his earlier poems ... Keats set out to write like a man, to pass beyond the feminine style, which he associated with the "Chamber of Maiden Thought."' ('Keats's Realm of Flora', p.94).
34 Note Keats's great disappointment when it became evident that Kean would not be able to play the part: 'I had hoped to give Kean another

opportunity to shine. What can we do now? There is not another actor of Tragedy in all London or Europe ...' (letter to Fanny Keats, 28 August 1819; *Letters*, p. 284).

35 Brown, *Life of John Keats*, ed. Bodurtha and Pipe, pp.54–5.

36 Aileen Ward, *John Keats: The Making of a Poet*, p. 304.

37 *New British Theatre* (1814), I.216.

38 Daniel P. Watkins, 'A Reassessment of Keats's *Otho the Great*', pp.56 and 55.

39 Catherine Burroughs, 'Acting in the Closet', p.130. A fundamental flaw in Burroughs's argument is her treatment of Otho as a 'closet' drama – which it definitely was not.

40 In a reading of the play which establishes interesting parallels with *Lamia*, Charles J. Rzepka interprets Ludolph's self-delusion as a rejection of 'the other characters' facility in adjusting their roles to shifting expectations'. As a result, Rzepka argues, 'Ludolph becomes obsessed with maintaining a fictional self – the devoted bridegroom – from which he cannot quite withdraw without, literally, losing all sense of self, i.e., dying' ('*Theatrum Mundi* and Keats's *Otho the Great*: "The Self in Saciety"', p.44). My own analysis, however, demonstrates the extent to which I disagree with Rzepka's reading of Otho as a character who is 'unaffected by the expectations of the world at large' and who is thus 'secure in his own identity' (p.43).

41 Julie A. Carlson notes that the 'fantasy behind Ludolph's ravings is that he can turn back the hands of time: he seeks to restore the imbalance of male power, when men were tyrants and right was might, not a question of consent'. See *In the Theatre of Romanticism*, p.186.

42 Ross, 'Beyond the Fragmented Word', p.111.

# 5
# Lord Byron
## *Manfred* and the closet drama

I am acquainted with no immaterial sensuality so delightful as good acting. (Byron, 1814)[1]

But dearly do we pay all our life after for this juvenile pleasure, this sense of distinctness. When the novelty is past, we find to our cost that instead of realizing an idea, we have only materialized and brought down a fine vision to the standard of flesh and blood. We have let go a dream, in quest of an unattainable substance. (Lamb, 1812)[2]

## I

Any attempt to engage critically with the dramas, or closet dramas, produced by the Romantic poets must initially attempt to examine the relationship between the works themselves and the status of contemporary theatre and the issues and debates its prominence gave rise to. It is clear that the period spanning from the late eighteenth to early nineteenth centuries was one in which theatrical performance thrived and it is also well known that all of the canonical male Romantic poets produced one or more plays which were either performed or intended for performance upon the stage. However, it is also the case that many writers of the period – particularly those often associated with these poets and their circles – subscribed to what has been termed the period's anti-theatrical prejudice. Even William Hazlitt, an inveterate and generally enthusiastic theatregoer, could sometimes express the opinion that the best plays (as represented by the work of Shakespeare) inevitably lost much of their appeal in performance: 'the reader of the plays of Shakespeare is almost always disappointed in seeing them acted; and, for our own parts, we should never go to see them acted, if we could help it.'[3] A frequent opposition in much Romantic drama criticism is that between the play performed and the play read – and it is invariably the reading experience which is celebrated as the most worthwhile and the one which is able to provide the greatest insight into the author's intentions and sensibility without the apparently extraneous distractions of stage business and the physical presences of the actors. Yet Hazlitt's mode of expression is revealing – he would not go to see Shakespeare acted 'if [he] could help it': the implication is that theatre going is a kind of compulsion, a desire which has to be pursued but which inevitably leads to feelings of dissatisfaction.

A similar compulsion is perhaps in evidence in the tendency of the Romantic poets to criticise contemporary theatre and yet at the same time to reveal a sustained interest in it, an interest which, as has been noticed above, often finds its way into their own artistic production. One of the most interesting and revealing manifestations of this ambiguous relationship with the theatre is the propensity of these poets to write 'closet' plays which, in the manner of Milton's *Samson Agonistes*, are intended for the reader rather than the spectator. In writing in this form, the poet satisfies the dramatic impulse whilst at the same time maintaining the hierarchy of the text which is read over that which is performed. One such closet drama is Byron's *Manfred*, which signals its generic intentions in its subtitular self-categorisation as 'A Dramatic Poem'. The *Edinburgh Review* noted the appositeness of this definition in its 1817 review of the poem: 'This piece is properly entitled a dramatic Poem – for it is merely poetical, and it is not at all a drama or play in the modern acceptation of the term.'[4] Byron's text, even though it utilises the conventions of written versions of dramatic texts, both announces itself as different from the script of a play to be performed and is immediately perceived as such by a reader aware of the 'modern acceptation' of what constitutes a stage play. Despite this overt and implicit rejection of actual stage performance, however, Philip Martin rightly stresses that 'Although it is one of the most unstageable of his dramas, *Manfred* nevertheless draws on Byron's experience of theatre more extensively than any other play he wrote'.[5] Whilst seemingly denying the physical presence of the stage, Byron evokes it, returning to it with the compulsion hinted at in the extract from Hazlitt quoted earlier; a compulsion which leads either to the paradox of a written text which constantly evokes its own unattainable performance or, in the theatre itself, to the similarly paradoxical situation of the 'immaterial sensuality' presented by bodily performance: the text summons its absent performance, the performance evokes the absent purity of the text. This chapter aims to explore these paradoxes slightly further and to examine the ways in which an inevitable concern with the body in performance relates to a discourse of gender difference. Before we focus in more detail on *Manfred*, though, it is necessary to say something more about the terms which were used during this period to discuss theatre and the anti-theatrical prejudice.

## II

One objection which writers of this period constantly raise against the theatre concerns its increasing use of theatrical effects such as scenery, music and general stage spectacle, effects initially associated with pantomime, melodrama and opera but which were gaining ground in all varieties of theatrical production.[6] In an essay, 'On the Opera', from 1818, Hazlitt describes the problems he experiences when confronted by what he sees as the excesses of certain kinds of theatrical experience:

The multitude and variety of objects distracts the attention ... The powers of the mind are exhausted, without being invigorated ... The mind is made 'the fool of the senses', and cheated of itself ... It is a species of intellectual prostitution; for we can no more receive pleasure from all our faculties at once than we can be in love with a number of mistresses at the same time.[7]

Underlying Hazlitt's discussion is, of course, an essential opposition of mind and body but it is also clear that this opposition is seen in sexual terms and in terms which are gendered in a complex way. The mind is seen as an active 'power' which is in danger of being over-powered and rendered passive through the accumulative effect of sensory stimulation. Such stimulation leads to exhaustion rather than invigoration, the implication being that Hazlitt's masculine intellect is threatened with an emasculating feminine passivity: the masculine spectator is placed within a disempowered feminine subject position where a sense of self-identity is disconcertingly denied (it is 'cheated of itself'). This tendency in Hazlitt's reading of the situation is further revealed in his description of the ensuing 'intellectual prostitution' where, like a (female) prostitute who depends for her life upon the exploitative demands of a large number of (male) customers, the (male) spectator is forced to give himself up to a variety of different (feminine) sensual attractions. In terms of the discourse of gender, one could argue, the experience is unsettling for Hazlitt because it leads to an unnerving reversal of the usual gender relationships –

and, in light of this, it is significant that Hazlitt rhetorically reverses this reversal at the end of the passage by transforming his image of the threatened male spectator from that of a disempowered intellectual prostitute into that of an autonomous and self-controlled Don Juan (who is asked to be 'in love with a number of mistresses at the same time').

Despite this concluding rhetorical escape clause, the experience of operatic theatre is clearly one which Hazlitt sees in terms which suggest a challenge to the masculine self-assertion of the spectator whose intellectual abilities are rendered impotent through a bombardment of sensual spectacle. Central to Hazlitt's account is the fear of being placed in a situation which is analogous to that of the prostitute, and it is by probing the significance of this depiction of the prostitute slightly further that we can begin to see the wider implications of the theatrical prejudice itself. Sonia Hofkosh has convincingly demonstrated the ways in which (male) Romantic writers used the image of the prostitute to explore the nature of their own profession, one which is crucially implicated in the production of 'self': 'The author's "character and property" are inscribed in a single gesture of writing that is simultaneously an act of identification and of appropriation – a drawing of boundary lines.'[8] Because of the implicit and/or explicit autobiographical nature of Romantic writing, the production of 'self' and the production of the text are co-existent: the self produces the text and is produced by it simultaneously. However, the vicissitudes of the marketplace, where both author and text have to 'live', mean that the 'self' which is produced is at the mercy of both commerce and the reader (two forces which are, of course, inevitably linked). In this way, the situation of the writer becomes strangely analogous to that of the prostitute:

the prostitute makes indifferent distinctions between bodies and business: she is her own commodity. Selling herself, she conflates private and public, subject and object, profiting from the very commerce that depersonalizes and alienates her. Prostitution serves in this period as a general metaphor for the debasement of literary practice into a promiscuous professionalism that renders authorship meaningful only by disempowering the author *as such*.[9]

It is interesting to note that the examples Hofkosh cites from Wordsworth's *Prelude* to substantiate her claim about the poet's use of the image of the prostitute are also closely linked with the image of the theatre – Wordsworth describes how he has observed a 'sportive infant' incongruously placed among the morally corrupt frequenters of the London playhouses:

> There, too, conspicuous for stature tall
> And large dark eyes, beside her infant stood
> The mother; but, upon her cheeks diffused,
> False tints too well accorded with the glare
> From play-house lustres thrown without reserve
> On every object near.[10]

Drawing upon the established association of playhouses and prostitutes, Wordsworth develops it here to suggest that, in their ability to throw their 'lustres' indiscriminately 'without reserve / On every object near', the playhouse and the prostitute share an essential similarity.[11] If, as Hofkosh suggests, Wordsworth implicitly establishes a parallel between writer and prostitute, then the theatre too becomes an image of the author's feminised loss of masculine self-control and reserve that is represented in the first instance by the image of the woman herself.

Hazlitt, as a spectator in the theatre, feels himself to be in danger of becoming a feminised victim of 'intellectual prostitution'; Wordsworth sees in the images of both theatre and prostitute a terrifying version of what he, as writer, might become: a sullied commodity devoid of any intrinsic value or meaning. For the Romantic writer, the play as a genre perhaps embodied most clearly the fears and doubts caused by the new relationship between commerce and literature: if an author's work creates that author's sense of self, and acts as its guarantee of validity, how can this self survive the processes of theatrical production and reception? In a system which necessarily and overtly relies upon elements in excess of the writer's own words (on scenery, music and the physical presence and abilities of the actors, for instance), how can the author's text, and the self it produces, retain its integrity? One answer to this dilemma is, of course, the closet drama, the 'dramatic poem' such as *Manfred*, which, whilst having the apparent accoutrements of the drama, provides the author with the seemingly more controllable act of reading as its site of reception. In this way the Romantic poet attempts to reassert a masculine control against the threat of a feminine diffuseness of meaning generated during performance. The dramatic poem is not, of course, an answer to the general fears identified by Hofkosh

– all kinds of writing, including the closet drama, are exposed to the instabilities of commerce – but it does indicate one of the reasons why writers might have been drawn to this poetic genre.

There are perhaps further reasons for the theatrical 'compulsion' identified earlier in this chapter: writing in *The Prelude*, for instance, Wordsworth associates the experience of the theatre, in its simplest and most basic forms, with formative stages in his own childhood. Despite his evident disgust and dismay at the corruption and immorality pertaining to the theatre environment, Wordsworth reveals an enthusiasm for the theatre itself and proceeds to make a distinction between its qualities at the time he is recording and at the time of writing the poem, a distinction which leads him to further contemplation of the travelling theatres of his youth:

> Enchanting age and sweet!
> Romantic almost, looked at through a space,
> How small, of intervening years! For then,
> Though surely no mean progress had been made
> In meditations holy and sublime,
> Yet something of a girlish child-like gloss
> Of novelty survived for scenes like these;
> Enjoyment happily handed down from times
> When at a country-playhouse, some rude barn
> Tricked out for that proud use, if I perchance
> Caught, on a summer evening through a chink
> In the old wall, an unexpected glimpse
> Of daylight, the bare thought of where I was
> Gladdened me more than I had been led
> Into a dazzling cavern of romance,
> Crowded with Genii busy among works
> Not to be looked at by the common sun. (7.441–57)

There is a revealing ambiguity in this passage: Wordsworth is half celebrating and half excusing his attraction to the theatre. On the one hand he sees it as a sign of immaturity, an indication that, although he has achieved a certain degee of 'holy and sublime' sophistication, he still retains the naive pleasures of the child; on the other hand he evidently records these childish pleasures with enthusiasm and attaches great importance to them – an importance which is, of course, even more obvious when placed in the context of the poem as a whole where the insights of childhood guarantee the veracity of the adult poet's imaginative powers. The theatre is, then, both a dangerously deceptive (and perhaps corrupt and corrupting) place and one which ironically takes the poet back to the spontaneous enjoyments and insights of childhood. It is significant that Wordsworth registers this ambiguity in gendered terms: the theatre is attractive because it still possesses a 'girlish child-like gloss of novelty'. The normally positive Wordsworthian connotations of 'child-like' are countered by the obviously critical 'girlish', as if to register the fact that his childhood susceptibility to the representations of stage illusion were a feminine weakness which his masculine adult self has to disown but cannot quite do so.

Wordsworth is not alone in forging links between the theatre and the innocence (or ignorance) of childhood where the masculine intellect was subordinated to the feminine senses. In a *London Magazine* article from 1820, Hazlitt discusses the minor theatres of London and suggests that they form a bridge between the most sophisticated metropolitan theatre and

its first rudiments and helpless infancy. With conscious happy retrospect, they lead the eye back, along the vista of the imagination, to the village barn, or travelling booth, or old-fashioned town-hall, or more genteel assembly-room, in which Momus first unmasked to us his fairy revels, and introduced us, for the first time in our lives, to that strange anomaly in existence, that fanciful reality, that gay waking dream, *a company of strolling players!*[12]

Hazlitt effectively parallels the history of the theatre with his own psychological and imaginative development; as a child he witnesses theatre in its own 'first rudiments and helpless infancy', moving on in adulthood to an appreciation of the most sophisticated and fully developed London drama. Like Wordsworth's account of the childhood/theatre relationship in *The Prelude*, this suggests that an appreciation of the theatre is inextricably linked with the sources of imaginative perception within the adult; more obviously than Wordsworth, however, Hazlitt intimates that the insights initiated by early dramatic experiences can be matured into a suitably 'adult' pleasure. Charles Lamb, on the other hand, whilst also an enthusiastic theatregoer, famously held that the theatre inevitably failed to do justice to the greatest works of dramatic literature – namely the tragedies of Shakespeare – and suggested that these plays could be successfully performed only in the theatre of the mind. He too associates the theatre with immature and childish pleasures, noting the pleasure that early theatre trips gave to him:

But dearly do we pay all our life after for this juvenile pleasure, this sense of distinctness. When the novelty is past, we find to our cost that instead of realising an idea, we have only materialized and brought down a fine vision to the standard of flesh and blood. We have let go a dream, in quest of an unattainable substance.[13]

In this rejection of 'juvenile pleasures' Lamb implicitly introduces the motif of the Fall into his deployment of the mind–body binary opposition. If we succumb to the temptations of the theatre we will 'pay all our life' for the sin of subjugating the mind to the body, succumbing to the feminine lures of the senses instead of obeying the rules of masculine reason. That the narrative of the Fall – and the discourse of gender that accompanies it – provides a subtext to Lamb's account of the theatre is suggested by his repeated reference to the Miltonic/Biblical myth of Adam and Eve. In his (effectively racist) discussion of the effect of Othello's skin colour in performances of the play, for example, he notes that:

The error of supposing that because Othello's colour does not offend us in the reading, it should not offend us in the seeing, is just such a fallacy as supposing that an Adam and Eve in a picture shall affect us just as they do in the poem. But in the poem we for a while have Paradisaical senses given us, which vanish when we see a man and his wife without clothes in the picture.[14]

The main thrust of Lamb's argument is that the play as it is performed represents a fallen version of the play as written (and read) text: the intellectual or spiritual matters conveyed by the author of a written text are 'sullied and turned from their very nature' (to quote from elsewhere in the same essay) by the act of physical performance.[15] Yet whilst Lamb implies, on the one hand, that this difference is a result of textual difference (between text-as-reading and text-as-performance), on the other hand he suggests that it is caused by the inadequacies, or – to follow the analogy he himself uses – the fallen nature, of the spectators themselves. Whilst reading the reader is given (or, from a larger perspective, regains) 'Paradisaical senses' which are able to resist the temptations of flesh and blood; the theatre, however, acts as a reminder of human weakness as manifested in and through sexual desire. The dynamics of such a theatrical experience are clearly gendered, for masculine reason is seen to be compromised by the overpowering nature of the feminine senses in a way similar to the overpowering of Adam by Eve in *Paradise Lost*.[16]

From this brief survey of the comments made by a variety of Romantic writers on the challenges presented by their contemporary theatre, it can be seen that, in several different ways it was perceived as posing a 'feminine' threat to 'masculine' control, either in the image it offered of the male Romantic writer prostituting himself to the uncertainties of the marketplace or, more abstractly, as something which threatened to destabilise the binary opposition between mind and body, reason and the senses. At the same time, however, the works examined here all reveal elements of an attraction towards the theatre which manifests itself both in terms of sexual desire and in relation to an irrecoverable but intensely desired innocence often described in terms of childhood pleasure (Wordsworth's 'girlish child-like gloss / Of novelty'). What emerges from this is the insecurity of the male writers of the period as regards not only their professional (and commercial) status but also in relation to their position within the discourse of gender difference and sexual desire, in which an escape from tensions and ambiguities can be sought only in a pre-sexual childhood which is always already lost and the evocation of which only returns the author to the instabilities of the present.

### III

The Romantic preoccupation with the split between mind and body which informs and problematises much of the contemporary debate about the value and status of the theatre is a central concern of Byron's 'dramatic poem' *Manfred* which was first published in 1817. In the second scene of Act I, Manfred, is alone upon the cliffs of the Jungfrau mountain, despairing at the human condition, which he perceives to be a frustrating mixture of 'Half dust, half deity' (I.ii.40), and yearning for the possibility of an incorporeal freedom:

> Oh, that I were
> The viewless spirit of a lovely sound,
> A living voice, a breathing harmony,
> A bodiless enjoyment – born and dying
> With the blest tone that made me! (I.ii.52–6)[17]

Manfred's evocation of a 'bodiless enjoyment' corresponds significantly with the 'bodiless' reading of a dramatic text advocated by Lamb and others, a process of textual production which makes the action of the play 'viewless' and enables the reader to forget his (*sic*) body and bodily desires.

Manfred is attempting to escape the restrictions of mortal life and overcome the consequences of the crimes his Promethean sprit has impelled him to commit – most obviously the crime of incest and his responsibility for his sister Astarte's subsequent death. Throughout the play he meditates upon intellectual motives and aspirations rather than material actions and consequences, and the reader of this closet drama is implicitly invited to do likewise. Again, it is useful to relate this to Lamb's essay on Shakespeare in which he discusses the different effect the crimes of Shakespeare's characters produce in reading and performance:

in ... characters in Shakespeare so little do the actions comparatively affect us, that while the impulses, the inner mind in all its perverted greatness, solely seems real and is exclusively attended to, the crime is comparatively nothing. But when we see these things represented, the acts which they do are comparatively everything, the impulses nothing.[18]

*Manfred* directs the reader to the 'perverted greatness' of the epony-mous hero and not to the physical reality of the crimes he commits: like Manfred himself, the 'greatness' of the play can be recognised only if it remains in this sense 'viewless' and the reader recognises that it is the incorporeal 'impulses' that must be attended to and not the material conditions of their enactment or obstruction. Approached in this way, *Manfred* can be read productively at a meta-textual level, at a level where the aspirations of the hero are signifi-cantly paralleled by those of the play itself. As a 'dramatic poem' or closet drama *Manfred* necessarily refuses to be embodied in physical performance, aspiring to the state of a 'living' – but 'bodiless' – 'voice'. Philip Martin notes an interesting implication of this denial of the actor's role:

by banning its performance, the acting implicit in the text is preserved as [Byron's] own. To the reader accustomed to identifying the heroes of Byron's poetry with Byron himself, *Manfred*, by proposing a wholly new and fundamentally dramatic relationship between author and reader, transforms the poet into the actor: the drama presents Byron as Kean, fully responsible for the representation of the leading role.[19]

One would want to qualify this observation by saying that it is not Byron the man who is here performing the 'leading role' but 'Byron' as cultural and, more importantly, textual product for, if we return to the arguments of Sonia Hofkosh, we can suggest that Byron's desire for the control that the closet drama apparently offers is a result of the threat of uncertainty and instability that commerce and the marketplace present to authorial identity: in producing *Manfred* Byron is producing himself (as text and, less positively, as commodity) and the element of self-enactment noted by Martin is a strategy adopted in the (necessarily thwarted) quest for 'masculine' self-control.

Within the poem Manfred embarks upon another, ultimately related, quest which lacks any clear focus or object but which is clearly and crucially linked to his relationship with his sister Astarte. In Act II, scene ii, Manfred describes his sister and their early attachment:

> She was like me in lineaments; her eyes
> Her hair, her features, all, to the very tone
> Even of her voice, they said were like to mine;
> But soften'd all, and temper'd into beauty:
> She had the same lone thoughts and wanderings,
> The quest of hidden knowledge, and a mind
> To comprehend the universe: nor these
> Alone, but with them gentler powers than mine,
> Pity, and smiles, and tears, – which I had not;
> And tenderness – but that I had for her;
> Humility – and that I never had.
> Her faults were mine – her virtues were her own -
> I loved her, and destroy'd her! (II.ii.105–17)

Astarte, as she is presented by Manfred in this passage, appears as a feminised version of her brother and, moreover, as a feminised version of him which only has an existence in the past and the innocence of which is lost and lamented in the present. The situation is reminiscent of the 'girlish child-like' pleasures which have been lost by the adult Wordsworth in *The Prelude* and, like Wordsworth's response to his feminised past, Byron's relationship with Astarte is a complex one. Alan Richardson has attempted to classify it in accordance with Freud's theories of primary and secondary narcissism. He quotes Manfred's recollection of Astarte's qualities and notes that

Manfred's love necessarily destroys its object, because his end is not union with Astarte but the assimilation of her. As the infant's incorporation of the mother or aspects of the mother is founded in what psychoanalysis calls 'primary narcissism', the assimilation of a sister or lover (or both in one) follows a later narcissistic relation described by Freud in a passage that seems to echo Manfred's confession: 'When narcissistic gratification encounters actual hindrances, the sexual ideal may be used as a substitute gratification. In such a case a person loves (in conformity with the narcissistic type of object-choice) someone whom he was and no longer is, or also someone who possesses excellences which he never had at all'. In Romantic portrayals of either narcissistic relation, the goal remains constant: appropriation of feminine, maternal characteristics and functions.[20]

Richardson's comments are worth quoting at length because they make explicit the relationship between Manfred's (sexual and physical) desire for his sister and his implicit quest for a pre-sexual innocence (which is ironically depicted in the poem as incorporeal even though a Freudian reading would locate its source in the physical interactions of the mother–child dyad). Furthermore, Richardson demonstrates how this dual desire is situated within a contemporary discourse of gender difference and thus works to maintain masculine control and autonomy through the 'appropriation' and containment of feminine qualities.

Having said this, Richardson's argument fails to explain fully the complex nature of Manfred's dependence upon his sister: his passion might literally, within the play's narrative, have been responsible for Astarte's death but, as the drama unfolds, it is evident that she is far from being a spent force, and it is Manfred's death, and not hers, which retrospectively structures the narrative. Although Astarte does not herself at first appear within the poem, her part is, to use an apposite theatrical analogy, performed in the first scene by one of the spirits summoned by Manfred, and this performance is one which obviously troubles and disturbs his masculine self-control:

> *Seventh Spirit [appearing in the shape of a beautiful female figure].*
> Behold!
> *Man.* Oh God! if it be thus and *thou*
> Art not a madness and a mockery,
> I yet might be most happy, I will clasp thee,
> And we again will be –
> > *[The figure vanishes.*
> > My heart is crush'd!
> > *[MANFRED falls senseless. (I.i.188–91)*

This is not the reaction of someone who has safely 'appropriated' the femininity represented by Astarte: Manfred's sister remains a troubling presence within the poem as his desire for her remains even though there is no object to which it can be directed. The troubling otherness of her femininity is accentuated in her death where she effectively escapes any attempted acts of appropriation. If such acts had been successful, as Richardson suggests they have, then the poem would lose much of its tension and ambiguity: Manfred, as Richardson observes, needs to 'destroy' Astarte in order to confirm the self-sufficiency of his masculine self and yet throughout the drama there is a counteracting tendency on his part to revive the very person whose femininity would destroy him. In the fourth scene of Act II, Manfred calls upon Nemesis to 'uncharnel' the Phantom of Astarte (an interesting combination of the grossly corporeal and the immaterial which will be discussed in more detail in the next section) so that he can question her:

> Speak to me! though it be in wrath; – but say –
> I reck not what – but let me hear thee once –
> This once – once more!
> *Phantom of Astarte.*　　Manfred!
> *Man.*　　　　　　　　　　Say on, say on –
> I live but in the sound – it is thy voice!
> *Phan.* Manfred! To-morrow ends thine earthly ills.
> Farewell!
> *Man.*　　Yet one word more – am I forgiven?
> *Phan.* Farewell!
> *Man.*　　　　　Say, shall we meet again?
> *Phan.*　　　　　　　　　　　Farewell!
> *Man.* One word for mercy! Say thou lovest me.
> *Phan.* Manfred!
> 　*[The Spirit of ASTARTE disappears* (II.iv.148–55)

Until this point in the poem Manfred has been haunted by his ideal memory of Astarte – even the apparition of a spirit in the shape of his sister in the first scene filled him momentarily with a tentative hope for present and future happiness. Here, however, with the return of Astarte herself from the grave, he is offered no hope and all that his sister is able to announce to him in an oracular fashion is the fact of his own death. In one sense, Manfred might 'destroy' Astarte but the constant subtextual fear of the play is that in another sense her physical presence would more insidiously destroy him.

At a metatextual level, then, Manfred's ambiguous relationship with Astarte mirrors the text's troubled relationship with the possibility of its own performance. In its adoption of act and scene divisions, in its use of stage directions and contemporary conventions of staging and performance, *Manfred* constantly summons the ghost of its own bodily enactment which it has generically thwarted before the play begins (as Manfred has been responsible for his sister's death) by placing itself within the category of the 'dramatic poem'. The ghost of the performance none the less remains a disturbing presence which threatens to destabilise the author's control over his own textual production and leads to further strategies being deployed within the text in an attempt to retain the appearance of a masculine control.

## IV

Words divorced from their physical enactment are, within the closet drama, the means through which the author attempts to maintain autonomy over and in the text, yet, as has been seen, these words possess connotations which are constantly evoking the bodily other which the author attempts to suppress. In *Manfred* Byron provides an analogy for this process in Manfred's use of charms and spells – words which magically summon forth spirits, making the incorporeal take on a physical presence – which function as a sign of his (masculine) power but also, ironically, reveal, through his hysterical reactions to the apparitions they produce, his vulnerability to the femininity they represent. As if in acknowledgement of the ambiguous power located in these charms and spells (which exist on the borderland between mind and body), the text displays a revealing reticence in its treatment of them. In the first scene, for example, Manfred calls upon the 'spirits of the unbounded Universe' to appear:

> Ye, who do compass earth about, and dwell
> In subtler essence – ye to whom the tops
> Of mountains inaccessible are haunts,
> And earth's and ocean's caves are familiar things –
> I call upon you by the written charm
> Which gives me power over you – Rise!
> Appear! (I.i.31–7)

His attempts to summon the spirits continue with a 'sign' which remains unrevealed and an unvoiced 'curse': what is interesting is that in a play which insists upon remaining purely verbal, even certain words remain hidden from the reader. Manfred's 'written charm' remains unread by the reader as if it would lessen his power if it were to become the property of others – in a process that would be analogous to that whereby the author's power and self-identity are diminished when their own 'written charms', as represented by their books, become a public commodity. The stage direction near the beginning of the second scene of Act II performs a similarly reticent purpose in its depiction of the spell used by Manfred to call upon the Witch of the Alps: '*MANFRED takes some of the water into the palm of his hand, and flings it into the air, muttering the adjuration. After a pause, the WITCH OF THE ALPS rises beneath the arch of the sunbow of the torrent*' (II.ii after l.12). Again, the text refuses to provide the words which make up the 'adjuration' and this refusal guarantees the unstageable nature of the text for, even if the scene could be managed visually through ingenious stagecraft, it cannot finally be enacted if the words to be spoken are retained by the author. In a sense there is a revealing split between the levels of narrative and metanarrative here in that, whilst Manfred succeeds in making the Witch of the Alps visible, *Manfred* prevents its own bodying forth in performance.

In place of a performance which would diminish authorial control, one could suggest that Byron presents the reader with an unstageable mystery, a term which he himself uses later in his career as a generic category to describe his two plays (again closet dramas) *Cain: A Mystery* and *Heaven and Earth: A Mystery* (1821 and 1822). As is perhaps to be expected, Byron uses the term 'mystery' in an ironic and complex fashion, both evoking and transgressing the dramatic traditions he is calling upon. In his Preface to *Cain* he writes that:

The following scenes are entitled 'A Mystery' in conformity with the ancient title annexed to dramas upon similar subjects, which were styled 'Mysteries or Moralities'. The author has by no means taken the same liberties with his subject which were common formerly, as may be seen by any reader curious enough to refer to those very profane productions, whether in English, French, Italian, or Spanish.

There is a provocative irony at work here – for, whilst Byron's drama generally resists the temptations of lewd or satirical interludes, its general theme, as evinced in the central meeting between Cain and Lucifer, is one which provides a sustained and 'profane' attack on central tenets of Christianity. This departure from the original nature of Mystery plays was noted, for example, by the *Quarterly Review* in 1822:

The drama of 'Cain', Lord Byron himself has thought proper to call a 'Mystery', – the name which, as is well known, was given in our country, before the reformation, to those scenic representations of the mysterious events of our religion, which, indecent and unedifying as they seem to ourselves, were perhaps the principal means by which a knowledge of those events was conveyed to our rude and uninstructed ancestors. But except in the topics on which it is employed, Lord Byron's Mystery has no resemblance to those which it claims as its prototypes. These last, however absurd and indecorous in their execution, were at least, intended reverently.[21]

Byron's 'Mystery', then, is one which, in the eyes of this reviewer at least, works to destroy the mystery of religion by profanely and irreverently setting them forth within a play. Yet, without entering upon a detailed analysis of the play, one can see that, whilst the play does certainly challenge established religion, it none the less maintains its sense of 'mystery'. At one point, for example, Lucifer is describing to Cain the abilities possessed by immortal spirits:

> With us acts are exempt from time, and we
> Can crowd eternity into an hour,
> Or stretch an hour into eternity:
> We breathe not by a mortal measurement –
> But that's a mystery. (I.i.531–6)

This is satanic (and Byronic) humour: an allusion to the 'mysteries' which are both transgressed and yet maintained, for, whilst the orthodoxies of religious creed are challenged, the reality of a spiritual existence is not. The form of the drama plays its part in this maintenance of mystery in that, unlike the Mystery plays, it is unperformable in any conventional way – as the opening of the second act demonstrates:

> SCENE I. – *The Abyss of Space*
> *Cain.* I tread on air and sink not; yet I fear
> To sink. (II.1.1–2)

*Cain*, like *Manfred*, is essentially a closet drama and, in this way if no other, reveals an ironically conservative force which potentially aligns it with the sentiments expressed by Hannah More in the Advertisement to her (closet) *Sacred Dramas chiefly intended for Young Persons*: 'It would not be easy, I believe, to introduce Sacred Tragedies on the

English Stage. The scrupulous would think it profane, while the profane would consider it dull.'[22] More here reveals fears about the reception of religious sentiment when performed within the context of the theatre, a fear that Byron reveals in *Manfred* (and, as Sonia Hofkosh argues, other Romantic writers reveal in their own poems) in relation not to the Word of God but to the words which constitute the sense of an authorial self. In *Cain*, as in *Manfred*, Byron attempts to retain authorial control through the creation of mystery.

An element of mystery is, of course, a crucial component of any gothic text and it is as an essentially gothic narrative that *Manfred* is often read. The supernatural in various manifestations – such as ghosts, strange warning signs or, even, visits from the devil – are a common occurrence within gothic in all its forms, be it drama, novel or poem. Yet, what makes the gothic particularly distinctive is that this element of the supernatural inevitably exists alongside an often almost obsessive interest in the grotesquely, perversely or putrescently physical: rotting corpses, charnel houses, graves and crimes of unthinkable depravity and violence (often of a sexual nature) are frequently either hinted at or, as is perhaps more often the case, described in graphic detail. One way of interpreting this odd confrontation of the spiritual and the bodily is to see the former as providing some kind of protection against the implications of the latter. In an analysis of the gothic which ultimately relates to the interactions of social class, for example, Michel Foucault interprets the gothic obsession with unthinkable crime as a way of making the actuality of such crime less of a perceived threat:

a whole new literature of crime developed: a literature in which crime is glorified, because it is one of the fine arts, because it can be the work only of exceptional natures, because it reveals the monstrousness of the strong and powerful, because it reveals villainy is yet another mode of privilege: from the adventure story to de Quincey, or from the *Castle of Otranto* to Baudelaire, there is a whole aesthetic rewriting of crime, which is also the appropriation of criminality in acceptable forms.[23]

This notion of 'the appropriation of criminality in acceptable forms' is extremely close to a description of what Charles Lamb was suggesting takes place when one reads (rather than sees) Shakespeare: our attention is upon the 'exceptional natures' of the criminals and not upon the unacceptable reality of their crimes. According to this reading, just as the closet drama contains and controls unacceptable elements which would be unleashed in performance, so the gothic text contains and controls the outrages it ostensibly depicts by 'aesthetically rewriting' them into a form which is socially acceptable. In our reading of *Manfred*, however, we have frequently observed that such control is frequently threatened or undermined, and Jeffrey N. Cox suggests that something very similar is evident in gothic drama as a genre. He quotes Foucault's comments on the gothic and proceeds to observe that:

In Foucault's version, the Gothic is a tactic of containment, a way for hegemonic social and cultural forces to combat the popular appeal of crime. However, the Gothic drama does not seem so much an art of containment as that of display; its strange 'jumble' of forms does not so much contain one ideological vision as place them within a generic struggle, offering a kind of Bakhtinian heteroglossia.[24]

It is in terms of such a 'generic struggle' that we need to read *Manfred*, a struggle which is inevitably located within a discourse of gender difference.

In dealing with this generic and ideological struggle within *Manfred* it is useful to return to the opposition observed earlier between what could be termed the supernatural or spiritual on the one hand and that which can be described as the horror of the bodily and physical on the other. In her book *Powers of Horror*, Julia Kristeva attempts to probe the cultural and psychoanalytic resonances of the horror caused by those things which are perceived as 'abject'. The most obvious sources of abjection are things such as corpses, blood and other bodily fluids which contribute so obviously to the gothic genre yet Kristeva none the less insists upon a larger and more inclusive definition of the term which has further implications for Byron's poem:

It is ... not lack of cleanliness or health that causes abjection but what disturbs identity, system, order. What does not respect borders, positions, rules. The in-between, the ambiguous, the composite. The traitor, the liar, the criminal with a good conscience, the shameless rapist, the killer who claims he is a saviour ... Any crime, because it draws attention to the fragility of the law, is abject, but premeditated crime, cunning murder, hypocritical revenge are even more so because they heighten the display of such fragility. He who denies morality is not abject; there can be grandeur in amorality and even in crime that flaunts its disrespect for the law – rebellious, liberating, and suicidal crime. Abjection, on the other hand, is immoral, sinister, scheming, and shady: a terror that dissembles, a hatred that smiles, a passion that uses the body for barter instead of inflaming it, a debtor who sells you up, a friend who stabs you.[25]

Manfred is a criminal *par excellence*, a figure who transgresses the laws of society in his relationship with his sister and in the general pursuit of forbidden knowledge: as someone who has crossed the borders of what is socially acceptable he 'disturbs identity, system, order' and reveals to the reader of the drama the potential 'fragility of the law'. Does this then render him an object of abjection, a being who provokes in the reader a sense of the other which, whilst it possesses a fascination for the reader must be cast out for his or her self-identity to be maintained? The question is a difficult one in that, throughout the play, Manfred struggles to present himself as an example of what Kristeva clearly excludes from the category of the abject: 'He who denies morality is not abject; there can be grandeur in amorality and even in crime that flaunts its disrespect for the law.' It is in these terms that Manfred attempts to establish himself as a satanic or Promethean or Faustian hero who becomes heroic in his rejection of the moral codes that guide the rest of society. When, for example, in the first scene of Act II the Chamois Hunter suggests to Manfred that he should adopt the ways of Christian 'patience' as an answer to his problems, Manfred responds haughtily with

> Patience and patience! Hence – that word was made
> For brutes of burden, not for birds of prey;
> Preach it to mortals of a dust like thine, –
> I am not of thine order. (II.i.35–8)

Yet Manfred's problem throughout the play is that he is unable to achieve successfully this elevated state – the reply to the Chamois Hunter, for instance, sits ironically alongside a passage from one of Manfred's soliloquies in the preceding scene:

> How beautiful is all this visible world!
> How glorious in its action and itself!
> But we, who name ourselves its sovereigns, we,
> Half dust, half deity, alike unfit
> To sink or soar, with our mix'd essence make
> A conflict of its elements, and breathe
> The breath of degradation and of pride. (I.ii.37–43)

Manfred is at least 'half' composed of the same dust as the Chamois Hunter whom he rejects and, in his recognition of his own 'mix'd essence', becomes an example of the 'in-between, the ambiguous, the composite' in which Kristeva locates the abject.

It was suggested earlier that Manfred's desire for Astarte could be read, in terms of primary and secondary narcissism, as an attempt to return to the mother–child dyad via a narcissistic appropriation of the feminine. Yet it was also observed that Astarte's presence produced something akin to terror in her brother: when Nemesis evokes the Phantom of Astarte, his use of the verb 'uncharnel' hints at a gross physicality which rehearses in miniature the tension revealed within gothic between the mysterious/supernatural and the physical/horrible – and it also repeats in different terms Manfred's own 'mix'd essence' of 'deity' and 'dust'. This ambiguous response to Astarte can also be related to Kristeva's notion of the abject in a way which links it to our earlier reading. Kristeva argues that, within the individual, the abject first comes into being as the child breaks away from the mother–child dyad in the very first stages of the process which will lead to the constitution of its sense of self. The abject manifests itself before the child enters the realm of language and the Symbolic and registers her/his attempts to separate her/his body and bodily functions from those of the mother:

The abject confronts us … within our personal archeology, with our earliest attempts to release the hold of *maternal* entity even before ex-isting outside of her, thanks to the autonomy of language. It is a violent, clumsy breaking away, with the constant risk of falling back under the sway of a power as securing as it is stifling … [The child pursues] a reluctant struggle against what, having been the mother, will turn into an abject. Repelling, rejecting; repelling itself, rejecting itself. Ab-jecting.[26]

Within this interpretative framework we can begin to understand Manfred's ambiguous relationship not only with Astarte but also with himself: both he and his sister (and the relationship between them) can be related to this initial occurrence of the abject, an occurrence which clearly places the dynamics of the play within the discourse of gender difference. Alan Richardson saw the 'appropriation of feminine, maternal characteristics and functions' as the 'goal' of a colonising Romantic masculinity: here such attempts at appropriation can be seen in terms of the far more complex simultaneous desire and repulsion registered by the abject – the maternal/feminine is threatening because it acts as a reminder of the time before the autonomous masculine self had been established.

It has been suggested that one way in which *Manfred* attempts to deal with certain aspects of this threat is by recourse to a sense of 'mystery', and this is one aspect of the poem that was noted by the *Edinburgh Review*:

If we were to consider it as a proper drama, or even as a finished poem, we should be obliged to add, that it is far too indistinct and unsatisfactory. But this we take to be according to the design and conception of the author. He contemplated but a dim and magnificent sketch of a subject which did not admit of more accurate drawing, or more brilliant colouring. Its obscurity is part of its grandeur; – and the darkness that rests upon it, and the smoky distance in which it is lost, are all devices to increase its majesty, to stimulate our curiosity, and to impress us with deeper awe.[27]

The 'indistinct' quality that the reviewer detects in the poem can clearly be related to ways in which the text of *Manfred* resists the means whereby its performance could be staged and therefore fails to achieve the status of 'a proper drama': the mystery and indistinctness are in this way an aspect of generic classification. Most obviously, however, the reviewer's comments signal to the educated reader of the *Edinburgh Review* the fact that Byron's poem is to be read according to the aesthetic demands of the sublime as described by Edmund Burke. In *A Philosophical Enquiry into the Origin of Our Ideas of the Sublime and Beautiful* (1757), Burke discusses the propensity of 'Obscurity' to produce a sublime effect:

To make any thing terrible, obscurity seems in general to be necessary. When we know the full extent of any danger, when we can accustom our eyes to it, a great deal of the apprehension vanishes ... No person seems better to have understood the secret of heightening, or of setting terrible things, if I may use the expression, in their strongest light by the force of a judicious obscurity, than Milton. His description of Death in the second book is admirably studied ... In this description all is dark, confused, terrible, and sublime to the last degree.[28]

According to the *Edinburgh Review*, Byron has deployed a similarly 'judicious obscurity' to that used by Milton in *Paradise Lost* and thus produced a work which takes its place as part of the masculine sublime in opposition to the feminine charms of the Burkean category of the beautiful. In yet another way, then, the mystery of *Manfred* – in its sublime aspect – becomes a counter to the encroachments of the desirable but none the less threatening feminine other.

In attempting to situate this alongside the ideas of Kristeva discussed earlier, one might be tempted to view the mysterious sublime as oppositional to the abject. However Kristeva describes the relation between the abject and the sublime as being more complex than a simple opposition:

The abject is edged with the sublime. It is not the same moment on the journey, but the same subject and speech bring them into being.

  For the sublime has no object either ... The 'sublime' object dissolves in the raptures of a bottomless memory ... I then forget the point of departure and find myself removed to a secondary universe, set off from the one where 'I' am – delight and loss. Not at all short of but always with and through perception and words, the sublime is *something added* that expands us, overstrains us, and causes us to be both *here*, as dejects, and *there*, as others and sparkling.[29]

Whereas *Manfred* appears to use the sublime as a counter to the abjection which it constantly evokes and yet denies, Kristeva's comments stress the essential similarity between these two apparently distinct aspects of human experience. Like the abject, the sublime relies for its effect upon an objectless desire and presents the individual subject with the vulnerability of his or her own sense of self. 'Memory' becomes a 'bottomless' well which sends the individual spiralling into a strange 'secondary universe' which, whilst it is reached 'through perception and words', is always in excess of those reassuring guarantors of the self. The sublime might offer the individual who experiences it a 'sparkling' otherness but, in so far as it fragments the perceiving self (which is 'both *here* ... and *there*'), it adumbrates the total disintegration threatened by the abject. In keeping with his tendency to live on the borders of different states, Manfred treads a fine line between the sublime and the abject, asserting the intoxicating power of the sublime whilst constantly dreading his descent into the annihilation of the abject.

  Manfred's sense of himself as half dust and half deity can be related to the doubleness of Kristeva's sublime: he is 'both *here* as deject and *there*, as other and sparkling'. The problem is that he mistakes this sense of sparkling otherness for his true 'self', converting it into a transcendent masculinity. It is such a belief in the masculine power of his own mind that Manfred, echoing Satan in *Paradise Lost*, asserts in the closing lines of Byron's poem:

> The mind which is immortal makes itself
> Requital for its own good or evil thoughts, –
> Is its own origin of ill and end –
> And its own place and time: its innate sense,
> When stripp'd of this mortality, derives
> No colour from the fleeting things without,
> But is absorb'd in sufferance or in joy,
> Born from the knowledge of its own desert. (III.iv.129–36)

Despite such confident masculine self-assertion, and his dismissal of the 'Demons' who appear to drag him to Hell, Manfred cannot defeat the prophecy of death voiced by the corpse/phantom of Astarte that his charmed words gave rise to in Act II. Sublime self-assertion is always anchored by a corresponding sense of dejection and both, ultimately, hover over the abyss of the abject. The drama ends, therefore, not with Manfred's triumph but with his ambiguous silence and the fact of his death which effectively reunites him with his sister. If this unstageable play were staged, the audience would be left with the presence of Manfred's corpse, a representation of the mortality and the abjection he both fought against and yet, ironically, desired.

## NOTES

1 *Byron's Letters and Journals*, IV.115.
2 Charles Lamb, 'On the Tragedies of Shakespeare, considered with reference to their Fitness for Stage Representation', in *Lamb as Critic*, p.87.
3 Hazlitt, 1815 review of *Richard II*, in *Complete Works*, V.222.
4 'Lord Byron's *Manfred*', *Edinburgh Review*, xxviii (August 1817), p.419.
5 Philip W. Martin, *Byron: A poet before his Public*, p.109.
6 For further discussion of this issue and related matters, see, for example, Frederick Burwick, *Illusion and the Drama*; Janet Ruth Heller, *Coleridge, Lamb, Hazlitt, and the Reader of Drama*, especially Chapters 1 and 2; Jeffrey N. Cox (ed.), *Seven Gothic Dramas*, Introduction; Julie A. Carlson, *In the Theatre of Romanticism*, Chapter 4; Daniel P. Watkins, *A Materialist Critique of English Romantic Drama*, Chapter 1; Timothy Webb, 'The Romantic Poet and the Stage: A Short, Sad History'.
7 Hazlitt, *Works*, XX.92–4; quoted in Heller, *Reader of Drama*, pp.39–40.
8 Sonia Hofkosh, 'A Woman's Profession: Sexual Difference and the Romance of Authorship', p.248.
9 Hofkosh, 'A Woman's Profession', p.257.
10 *The Prelude*, Book 5, 342–7; 1850 text from *The Prelude 1799, 1805 1850*, ed. Wordsworth, Abrams and Gill.
11 For a relevant and interesting discussion of the perceived relationship between theatres and prostitution at this time, see Julie A. Carlson, *In the*

    *Theatre of Romanticism*, pp.154–5.

12 *Works*, XVIII.292–3; quoted in Christopher Salveson, 'Hazlitt and Byron – Intermittent Affinities', p.123.

13 Lamb, 'On the Tragedies of Shakespeare', p.87.

14 Lamb, 'On the Tragedies of Shakespeare', p.98.

15 Lamb, 'On the Tragedies of Shakespeare', p.89.

16 See *Paradise Lost*, Book 8, ll.530ff for a discussion of the power of feminine 'passion' which is to be resisted by masculine reason.

17 All references to Byron's poems are taken from *Poetical Works*, ed. Frederick Page, new edition, corrected by John Jump.

18 Lamb, 'On the Tragedies of Shakespeare', p.95.

19 Philip W. Martin, *Byron: A Poet before his Public*, p.116.

20 Alan Richardson, 'Romanticism and the Colonization of the Feminine', pp.19–20.

21 *Quarterly Review*, 27 (July 1822), p.508; quoted in Philip Martin, *Byron: A Poet before his Public*, p.167.

22 Hannah More, *Sacred Dramas chiefly intended for Young Persons. The Subjects taken from the Bible. To which is added Sensibility, a Poem*, pp.vii–viii.

23 Michel Foucault, *Discipline and Punish*, pp. 68–9; quoted in Cox (ed.), *Seven Gothic Dramas*, p.31.

24 Cox (ed.), *Seven Gothic Dramas*, p.31.

25 Julia Kristeva, *Powers of Horror*, p.4.

26 Kristeva, *Powers of Horror*, p.13.

27 *Edinburgh Review*, XXVIII (August 1817), p.430.

28 Edmund Burke, *A Philosophical Enquiry into the Origin of our Ideas of the Sublime and the Beautiful*, Part Two, Section III, pp.54–5.

29 Kristeva, *Powers of Horror*, pp.11–12.

# 6

# Percy Bysshe Shelley

## *Prometheus Unbound*
## and the celebration of difference

### I

In June 1820, Baldwin's *London Magazine* published an enthusiastic advanced notice of Shelley's latest poem, *Prometheus Unbound*, in which the author paid particular attention to what he perceived to be the extreme contemporaneity of both the poet's ideas and the form of the poem itself: 'This poem is more completely the child of the *Time* than almost any other modern production: it seems immediately sprung from the throes of the great intellectual, moral and political *labour* of nations. Like the Time, its parent, too, it is unsettled, irregular, but magnificent.'[1] The relationship here expressed between the material conditions of a text's production and the nature of the text itself owes something perhaps to Shelley's own treatment of the subject in his Preface to the poem, and this is a topic which will be returned to later in the present chapter. More arresting initially is the reviewer's perception that the poem's 'magnificent' quality co-exists with (and is perhaps in part caused by) a correspondingly 'unsettled' and 'irregular' aspect, and that both the magnificence and the irregularity are intrinsically related to the contemporary political, social and intellectual climate which, it is claimed, gave birth to the poem.

The most obvious place to embark upon a consideration of these 'unsettled' and 'irregular' aspects of *Prometheus Unbound* is at the level of genre if only for the reason that Shelley's subtitular designation of the poem as 'A Lyrical Drama in Four Acts' is one which has caused much critical debate concerning the nature and effect of its generic classification.[2] An early unfavourable review of the poem in the *Quarterly Review* seized upon this generic issue to highlight what it took to be the obvious failure of the work as a whole, noting that Shelley 'has been pleased to call "Prometheus Unbound" a lyrical drama, though it has neither action nor dramatic dialogue'.[3] Even a

more sympathetic critic would have to concede that, from one perspective, this reviewer has a valid point for, considered as a 'drama',
*Prometheus Unbound* makes very strange reading. The first act presents us with Prometheus chained to the mountain side, his punish-
ment for defying Jupiter, where he remains for the duration of the
act. Any literal 'action' is made impossible by his physical confine-
ment and the majority of the 'dialogue' that takes place is between
the enchained Prometheus and the disembodied voices of his mother
Earth and the invisible Furies and Spirits who come either to taunt
or console him. What 'action' there is in this opening act of the poem
revolves around Prometheus's earlier 'curse', aimed at Jupiter, which
he 'recalls' – in the sense of both remembering and revoking.[4] If the
action of the first act can more properly be termed inaction, the
second act goes some way towards rectifying the apparent failure of
this 'drama': Asia, the lover from whom Prometheus is separated,
follows an invisible spirit towards the cave of the mysterious
Demogorgon where, after a rather cryptic question-and-answer session, she gains some kind of indirectly communicated (self-)knowl-
edge which leads, in the third act, to the downfall of Jupiter, the
liberation of Prometheus and the establishment of a democratic
Utopian vision in the final act of the poem. As the 'drama' moves
towards its climax, the central protagonists (if such they can be
termed) disappear from the stage (again, if it can be called such) and
the poem becomes a series of songs or lyrics performed by a variety
of allegorical and aetherial figures. Throughout, but particularly as
the poem develops, there is little of the narrative or character continuity one would expect from a dramatic text, despite the fact that
certain scenes clearly present themselves in dramatic terms. Conversely, it is these dramatic elements which prevent the poem from
being interpreted simply in terms of a 'lyric' (to use the other half of
Shelley's own generic classification). The result of this 'irregular' use
of genre is that many critics have discussed the poem in terms of a
shift from one genre or genres to another or others – thus, for example, the poem has been seen as moving from drama to lyric, or
tragedy to comedy (from Act I to Act IV); or pastoral (the beginning of Act II) to epic or romance (Asia's quest to seek Demogorgon as the act continues). Such criticism has revealed the rich
complexity of Shelley's text in a variety of ways, but what the wide
range of such responses has made evident is how the poem foregrounds in a distinctive manner the interactions of different genres

within the same work.

In his excellent discussion of the generic modulations of *Prometheus Unbound*, Stuart Curran begins by paying attention to Shelley's own generic classification alluding, as he does so, to an apparently similar instance in Wordsworth's work, noting that '[f]rom the very first Shelley alerts us to a mixture of modes even more purely antithetical than those of the *Lyrical Ballads*'.[5] The comparison with Wordworth is illuminating because, in the differences as much as in the similarities, it reveals much about the distinctiveness of Shelley's generic undertaking. In his exploration of genre in Shelley's work, Richard Cronin notes that a genre 'is a convention, a system of tacit agreements between the poet and his reader'[6] and it is precisely with this aspect of genre that Wordsworth engages in his Preface to the *Lyrical Ballads*. In a famous passage, Wordsworth outlines what he takes to be the relationship between poet and reader and describes how he is attempting to situate himself and his poetry within such a relationship:

It is supposed, that by the act of writing in verse an Author makes a formal engagement that he will gratify certain known habits of association; that he not only apprizes the Reader that certain classes of ideas and expressions will be found in his book, but that others will be carefully excluded ... I will not take it upon me to determine the exact import of the promise which by the act of writing in verse an Author, in the present day makes to his Reader; but I am certain, it will appear to many persons that I have not fulfilled the terms of an engagement thus voluntarily contracted ... I hope therefore the Reader will not censure me, if I attempt to state what I have proposed myself to perform; and also ... to explain some of the chief reasons which have determined me in the choice of my purpose: that at least he may be spared any unpleasant feeling of disappointment, and that I myself may be protected from the most dishonourable accusation which can be brought against an Author, namely, that of an indolence which prevents him from endeavouring to ascertain what is his duty, or, when his duty is ascertained, prevents him from performing it.[7]

Wordsworth begins by noting that, from the reader's perspective, the volume of poetry that he has produced might be seen to constitute a breach of the normally expected contract which exists between author and audience, and that ill-informed readers of the poetry might feel that they had been misled by what he earlier terms his literary 'experiment'.[8] However, the remainder of the quotation offers a defence against such adverse criticism: Wordsworth argues that, whilst the reader might find much that is unexpected in the poetry, he, as a poet, has not been guilty of forsaking the 'duty' which pertains to that function and that, in the remainder of the 'Preface' he will effectively re-establish an 'engagement' between himself and his reader by outlining the intentions which lie behind his poetic performance. Seen in this light, the 'Preface' represents a revised or rewritten version of the 'system of … agreements between the poet and his reader' that Richard Cronin writes of in relation to the function of genre. Wordsworth makes explicit what Cronin sees as 'tacit' but he is, none the less, still ultimately concerned with a stable and constant poet–reader correspondence.

In terms of the genre of *Lyrical Ballads*, what Curran terms the 'antithetical' modes of 'lyric' and 'ballad' are provided by the 'Preface' with a context in which their dialectically opposed differences can be synthesised and the reader is placed in a position where the 'lyrical ballad' can be approached, at least initially, as a distinct and intelligible genre in and for itself. The 'lyric', one might argue, has traditionally been associated with the private and introspective, with thought and feeling rather than action; the 'ballad', on the other hand, is traditionally linked with narrative and action, a genre which has little time for the depiction or analysis of psychological or emotional complexity. The *Lyrical Ballads* are poems which have stories to narrate but they are narratives which focus not so much upon action as feeling: 'the feeling therein developed gives importance to the action and situation, and not the action and situation to the feeling'.[9] Wordsworth's 'Preface' suggests that he is attempting to write a new form of narrative poetry, a new form of 'ballad' which is informed by an increased ('lyric') sensitivity to the thoughts and emotions of others. Thus, to take one example from many, 'Simon Lee, the Old Huntsman' appears at first to be a simple jaunty ballad which promises to relate an entertaining incident in the life of the eponymous hero. As the poem proceeds, however, no particularly noteworthy event is described – all that is revealed, with increasingly pathetic detail, is the extreme poverty of Simon's life. Towards the end of the poem the narrating voice intervenes to address the reader directly:

> My gentle reader, I perceive
> How patiently you've waited,
> And I'm afraid that you expect
> Some tale will be related.

> O reader! had you in your mind
> Such stores as silent thought can bring,
> O gentle reader! you would find
> A tale in everything.
> What more I have to say is short,
> I hope you'll kindly take it;
> It is no tale; but should you think,
> Perhaps a tale you'll make it. (69–80)

This poem, then, is not a 'tale' in the expected sense, but a new kind of 'tale': not a 'ballad' but a 'lyrical ballad' which replaces action and event with the insights offered by 'silent thought'. In this way 'Simon Lee' recapitulates and consolidates the programme outlined in the 'Preface' to the collection as a whole and directs the reader towards a new 'engagement' with the poet and the appreciation of a new generic category.

How, then, is this different to the 'antithetical' generic coupling of *Prometheus Unbound*'s 'lyrical drama'? An initial approach to the problem might reveal similarities between the generic strategies of the two poets. The 'drama', even more directly than the 'ballad', is concerned with physical action and the depiction of events taking place in the material world. The coupling of this genre with the 'lyric' might therefore suggest that Shelley is interested in the interactions of the internal and external, self and society, mind and body, and private and public. Such terms have been a constant concern of the present book, and each binary opposition has been seen to be gendered in terms of 'masculine' and 'feminine'. Read in this way, Shelley's 'lyrical drama' would be very similar generically to Byron's *Manfred: A Dramatic Poem*, a poem in which the perceived threat of the body or performance is controlled within the form of the 'closet' drama. Indeed, certain aspects of Shelley's 'Preface' to *Prometheus Unbound* would suggest that the effect of the 'lyrical drama' is to give precedence to the mind over the body and the internal over the external – as is illustrated by the section in which the poet discusses the poem's imagery: 'The imagery which I have employed will be found in many instances to have been drawn from the operations of the human mind, or from those external actions by which they are expressed.'[10] One would normally expect the imagery of a poem to be drawn from the external material universe and that such imagery would, perhaps, depict in some way the 'operations of the human mind'. Here Shelley reverses normal expectations and thus implicitly asserts the

primacy of the mind over the world it perceives – an assertion that is
perhaps to be expected from someone who states, in his 1819 essay
'On Life' that he subscribes 'to the conclusions of those philosophers, who assert that nothing exists but as it is perceived'.[11] In writing a 'lyrical' drama, therefore, Shelley could be seen to be stressing
the primary importance of individual perception in the construction
of what is usually termed external reality.

Yet it would be too simple to leave an examination of the genre of
*Prometheus Unbound* at this point. Shelley's belief in the primacy of
individual perception is not as clear cut as might at first appear: in
the essay 'On Life' he also writes positively of the state of being he
terms 'reverie'.

Those who are subject to the state of reverie feel as if their nature were
dissolved into the surrounding universe, or as if the surrounding universe were dissolved into their being. They are conscious of no distinction. And these are states which precede or accompany or follow an
unusually intense and vivid apprehension of life.[12]

In this state of 'reverie' the single, perceiving, 'masculine' self is
replaced by an amorphous being which dissolves into the surrounding universe and, as such, could clearly be gendered as 'feminine' in
a way similar to the state described by Keats when he writes of 'Negative Capability'. The essay 'On Life', therefore, clearly presents two
opposing ontological propositions, one of which relies upon a distinct and separate masculine subject position and one of which dis-
cards such masculine assertion of the self in favour of dissolution and
the eradication of distinction. In the 'Preface' to *Prometheus Unbound*
there is a similar and related opposition. Whilst the discussion of its
imagery quoted earlier might suggest that Shelley is emphasising the
primacy of mind over body in the poem, other sections indicate that
the relationship between the individual perceiving mind and the surrounding universe is more complex:

The great writers of our own age are, we have reason to suppose, the
companions and forerunners of some unimagined change in our social
condition or the opinions which cement it. The cloud of mind is dis-
charging its collected lightning, and the equilibrium between institu-
tions and opinions is now restoring or about to be restored.

This passage evidently presents a situation where writers are simply
the 'companions or forerunners' of any change in material 'social
conditions': they are able to influence 'opinion' but are obviously

subject to a force which one could perhaps term historical necessity. Shelley thus appears to acknowledge the crucial existence of social or historical or simply physical forces beyond the perceiving subject's control.

Like the poem itself as described by the *London Magazine* reviewer, the 'Preface' to *Prometheus Unbound* can also be seen as in some way 'unsettled' and 'irregular' and these irregularities again relate to the question of genre. In the 'Preface' to *Lyrical Ballads*, Wordsworth presents an argument which, whilst not without its difficulties, can be read as providing a cogent rationale for his generic choice and, in the poems which follow, the 'composite order' of genre (to use Stuart Curran's term) can be seen to have its own unified cogency. Shelley, on the other hand, presents a less logically coherent argument in his 'Preface' and the poem which follows refuses the synthesis of 'antithetical' modes achieved in the *Lyrical Ballads*. If the generic designation 'a lyrical drama' indicates a concern with the oppositions of mind and body, internal and external, and masculine and feminine, then, as will be seen, *Prometheus Unbound* resists the synthesis that the generic, ontological and social antitheses invite. Shelley's poem is one which strives to maintain and even re-establish the concept of difference even when this apparently leads to self-contradiction, logical impasse or paradox. At the beginning of this section it was noted that the reviewer in the *London Magazine* described *Prometheus Unbound* as 'the child of the Time': Shelley would probably have agreed with this assessment but, at the same time, he would also probably have disagreed. In the 'Preface' to *Prometheus Unbound* he famously observes that 'Poets, not otherwise than philosophers, painters, sculptors and musicians, are in one sense the creators and in another the creations of their age'. Shelley suggests that the imaginative perceiving subject – who is implicitly male – is in one sense the creator of the age in which he lives, and in another sense, its creation. In one sense the (male) poet is an active, masculine agent, in another he is a passive, feminine subject. *Prometheus Unbound* delights in such paradox, paradox which is deployed as a means to explore the nature and function of difference itself.

## II

In his discussion of what he interprets as 'controlled' 'inconsistencies' in Shelley's *A Defence of Poetry*, Richard Cronin notes that the poet's

'philosophical allegiances led him to distrust the impression of inconsistency transcended that paradox is designed to give, and to prefer
dialogue, whether explicit or implicit, as a means of registering contradictions'.[13] In broad and general terms one might say that the lyric
is monologic and the drama dialogic and thus that, in writing a lyrical drama, Shelley is opening the self-contained (masculine) certainty
of lyric to the (feminine) 'inconsistencies' and (self-)contradictions of
drama. However, more attention needs to be given to the notion of
paradox as it applies to Shelley's poem, particularly as Cronin himself later observes in his analysis of *Prometheus Unbound* that
'[p]aradox is a device that both tempts and frustrates logical reading,
and Shelley's diction plays with this situation'.[14] This would appear
to be a minor 'inconsistency' in Cronin's own argument, but the
problem is diminished if one accepts, as Cronin himself does in the
second quotation, that paradox need not simply be interpreted as
indicating 'inconsistency transcended'. A more useful definition of
the word as it relates to Shelley, and *Prometheus Unbound* in particular, is provided by Isobel Armstrong in her reading of the poem.
According to Armstrong:

> The structure of paradox enables negation, and affirmation, creation and
> denial, to be experienced simultaneously ... The new meaning it insists
> upon is a new category evolving out of a new relationship between is and
> is not which are continually changing places ... It is not merely a para-
> digm of the activity which forms intervals and interstices whose void for-
> ever craves fresh food, but it *is* that activity, constituting meaning in and
> through structure. It is a language discovering the void in the double
> sense of finding and exploring it, reaching out to possess the spaces it
> opens almost to the point of attenuation.[15]

This notion of paradox is dynamic rather than static, it is one which
maintains opposition and difference and yet at the same time refuses
to value one side of a binary over the other – indeed, whilst refusing
both synthesis and what Cronin sees as 'inconsistency transcended',
paradox here enables the writer to move beyond simple binaries in
order to establish an ever new series of oppositions. In this way the
facilitating 'language' of paradox suggests a move beyond the
impasse of western culture as described by Hélène Cixous (whose
ideas were deployed in this book's opening discussion of Coleridge).
Cixous, it will be remembered, observed that '[t]hought has always
worked by opposition':

By dual, *hierarchized* oppositions. Superior/Inferior. Myths, legends, books. Philosophical systems. Wherever an ordering intervenes, a law organizes the thinkable by (dual, irreconcilable; or mitigable, dialectical) oppositions. And all the couples of oppositions are *couples*. Does this mean something? Is the fact that logocentrism subjects thought – all of the concepts, the codes, the values – to a two-term system, related to 'the' couple man/woman?[16]

Paradox denies '*hierarchized* oppositions' and establishes relationships which are neither 'irreconcilable' (leading to stalemate) nor 'dialectical' (leading to synthesis). *Prometheus Unbound* maintains systems of difference (which can all, as Cixous explains, be seen to be related to the social construction of gender difference) and yet uses paradox as a means to challenge the repressive nature of logocentric or patriarchal binary oppositions.

The first two acts of Shelley's poem, for example, would seem to establish expectations of a traditionally conceived opposition between male/female, masculine/feminine: the first act concentrates upon Prometheus, the male hero renowned for his wisdom and intellectual prowess and foresight, whilst the second focuses on Asia, the female object of his love and identified with love and the feminine emotions in contrast to his more manly virtues. The experience of reading the play none the less complicates this potentially simple opposition. The play opens with Prometheus attempting to remember the defiant curse he had voiced against the tyrannical Jupiter and, in keeping with this, his first speech is full of an apparently aggressive and confrontational rhetoric. He awaits the hour which

> – As some dark Priest hales the reluctant victim –
> Shall drag thee, cruel King, to kiss the blood
> From these pale feet, which then might trample thee
> If they disdained not such a prostrate slave.
> Disdain? Ah no! I pity thee. (I.49–53)

As this extract progresses, though, it can be seen that the language of masculine violence and the desire for revenge modulates into what is effectively its opposite: the language of 'pity'. In his anticipation of the action of the metaphorical 'dark Priest', Prometheus is aligning himself implicitly with the same tyrannical behaviour as that adopted by his enemy and so, if his opposition to Jupiter is to be meaningful, he has to reject such violence in favour of a more liberating alternative. Yet, whilst this is the case, Prometheus's rejection of violence in favour of 'pity' challenges both generic and gender expectations. Marlon B. Ross notes that

> Shelley's male hero, then, must, like the chaste maiden of chivalry, learn to be physically inactive as he practices the arduous task of emotional integrity. He must learn the power that the heart can give the mind, and that the mind and heart together can give the other-directed self.[17]

Prometheus must temper his masculine intellect (the 'mind') with a feminine appreciation of emotion (the 'heart') and, through 'pity', learn to direct his sense of 'self' towards an understanding of the needs of others. However, in doing this, the 'male hero' becomes its opposite, that is, 'the chaste maiden' who is the passive object of the hero's desire. Thus Shelley presents his reader with a paradox in the sense recorded by Armstrong: Prometheus is the male hero of this tragedy and yet his heroic role appears to consist of his adoption of the passive feminine role of the heroine who is there to be acted upon rather than herself being a proactive agent.

The passivity of Prometheus is registered from the first lines of the last quotation from the play by the way in which he immediately places his faith not in his own actions but in the power of fate. He presents himself implicitly as being solely at the mercy of his own destiny and, unlike a traditional tragic hero, he refrains from fighting against this even in the opening scene of the first act. By the end of the act, his passive surrender to fate has become even more marked, leading to inaction and near-despair:

> This quiet morning weighs upon my heart;
> Though I should dream, I could even sleep with grief
> If slumber were denied not ... I would fain
> Be what it is my destiny to be,
> The saviour and strength of suffering man,
> Or sink into the original gulph of things ...
> There is no agony and no solace left;
> Earth can console, Heaven can torment no more. (I.813–20)

The word 'strength' sits awkwardly in this speech, for it is a quality which is seemingly absent from the protagonist who utters it; 'strength', in an acceptably masculine sense, is antithetical to the passivity and half-voiced desire for oblivion that Prometheus expresses. Conceived in terms of traditional, masculine, heroic drama, the 'saviour and strength of suffering man' would surely need to exhibit from the beginning those qualities which would fit him for the role;

by feminising his hero, Shelley challenges the reader's expectations of both masculinity and heroism.[18]

Prometheus's despair is not complete at the end of the first act because he still holds on to the belief that all 'hope' is 'most vain' save for that to be found in 'love' (I.808). This faith in the power of love (a force anticipated by Prometheus's own discovery of the power of 'pity' within himself) leads to the introduction of Asia in the second act, Prometheus himself disappearing from the play until after his liberation in Act III. The first scene of Act II is set in 'A lovely Vale in the Indian Caucasus', a suitably pastoral setting for the presentation of the poem's main female (and ostensibly feminine) protagonist. It is spring, and the season suggests a feeling of expectation as Asia awaits the arrival of her sister Panthea who is making her way to the Vale from Prometheus's side:

> This is the season, this the day, the hour;
> At sunrise thou shouldst come, sweet sister mine,
> Too long desired, too long delaying, come!
> How like death-worms the wingless moments crawl!
> The point of one white star is quivering still
> Deep in the orange light of widening morn
> Beyond the purple mountains; through a chasm
> Of wind-divided mist the darker lake
> Reflects it – now it wanes – it gleams again
> As the waves fade, and as the burning threads
> Of woven cloud unravel in pale air ...
> 'Tis lost! and through yon peaks of cloudlike snow
> The roseate sunlight quivers – hear I not
> The Aeolian music of her sea-green plumes
> Winnowing the crimson dawn?
>                                                   [Panthea *enters*]
>                         I feel, I see
> Those eyes which burn through smiles that fade in tears
> Like stars half quenched in mists of silver dew.
> Beloved and most beautiful, who wearest
> The shadow of that soul by which I live,
> How late thou art! the sphered sun had climbed
> The sea, my heart was sick with hope, before
> The printless air felt thy belated plumes. (II.i.13–34)

'Sick' with love, the only 'hope' that now remains in the world of *Prometheus Unbound*, Asia appears initially as the pining mistress, waiting impatiently but also impotently for news of her absent lover.

Her power to alter or affect her situation seems as limited as her power to influence the course of the sunrise she observes, her love for Prometheus appears to be a passive one which requires her to be perceived as an object of desire rather than as a desiring subject in her own right. Her 'soul' is given life only through the existence of Prometheus as her lover upon whom she is dependent in a conventionally feminine manner.

However, other aspects of this speech, and the scene as a whole, work against this simple allocation of feminine traits to a female protagonist. Whilst certain elements in the speech would suggest that Asia is an object of desire, her language ('How like death worms the wingless moments crawl!') often suggests an urgency which transgresses feminine decorum and intimates a more dynamic and potentially masculine passion. In a way which is continued throughout the remainder of the scene, Asia's desire for the absent Prometheus is partially transferred to her sister Panthea who is present: it is Panthea who is '[t]oo long desired' and who is '[b]eloved and most beautiful'. Panthea, bearing the 'shadow' of Prometheus, becomes effectively the immediate object of Asia's love and thus the female protagonist comes to perform a more active and masculine role in the expression of her desire. When Asia speaks of the 'eyes' which she can 'feel' and 'see' she is referring at one level to the eyes of Prometheus and, at another more immediate level, to those of Panthea which are before her. As she directs her gaze upon the eyes of the loved one in front of her she situates herself within a subject position which is implicitly masculine for, as Laura Mulvey observes: 'In a world ordered by sexual imbalance, pleasure in looking has been split between active/male and passive/female. The determining male gaze projects its phantasy on to the female figure which is styled accordingly.'[19] The fact that the objects of Asia's gaze are Panthea's eyes reinforces this point: the eyes of Panthea (and perhaps implicitly those of Prometheus) are transformed from organs which see (thus suggesting an autonomous and active subject position) to objects which are seen (implying the loss of such autonomy). Mulvey proceeds to suggest that the male gaze has structural implications within a text (she is specifically referring to filmic texts, but the implications of her argument possess a more general relevance): 'An active/passive heterosexual division of labour has similarly controlled narrative structure ... Hence the split between spectacle and narrative supports the man's role as the active one of forwarding the story, making things happen.'[20] The woman in traditional narrative is a 'spectacle' for the male protagonist, an object of desire who can do nothing to forward the narrative herself but who acts as an object of desire for the male protagonist who forwards the 'story' and thus brings about a narrative dynamic which works against the static spectacle offered by the woman. In *Prometheus Unbound*, though, this narrative structure is disrupted: the male hero is, as has been seen, rendered passive and the apparently passive heroine is transformed into an active, masculine force through the transforming power of her desire.[21] Looking deep into Panthea's eyes – 'Lift up thine eyes / And let me read thy dream' (II.i.55–6) – Asia enters into an erotic union with her sister/Prometheus and then, gaining a vision of Panthea's 'other dream' (II.i.132), observes a figure which disturbs the first dream and beckons her to 'Follow! follow!' (II.i.131). As she takes up the challenge offered by this call, Asia is fully transformed from passive femininity to active masculinity, becoming a 'forwarding' agent in the narrative dynamics of the poem. And, as Richard Cronin notes, this alteration is mirrored at a generic level, for in Act II 'poetry breaks out of a pastoral mode towards epic' as Asia commences her 'search for Prometheus' who has, in effect, become the passive object who inspires her quest.[22]

Marlon B. Ross observes this apparent inversion of gender roles between Asia and Prometheus but is none the less hesitant to ascribe to Shelley's text a complete victory over patriarchal norms. Ross's reservations are related to what he sees as 'her role in the poem as a reactive subject in the second act'.[23] In part this objection can be met by stating that, as has been already discussed, the normal masculine function within narrative is 'reactive' in that the male protagonist responds to the passive 'spectacle' offered by the female. However, in making his point, Ross refers the reader to a potentially more difficult and troubling passage from the end of Act I in which Prometheus describes the nature of his relationship with Asia:

> thou art far
> Asia! who when my being overflowed
> Wert like a golden chalice to bright wine
> Which else had sunk into the thirsty dust. (I.809–12)

For Ross, this speech is one which offers

a beautiful image, but none the less one which derives its potency from a limiting masculine perspective. His overflowing is the initial act, just as his repentance, his emotional overflowing, is the act that initiates the poem. The need to intensify and then fulfill his desire is what determines her form as a salvational chalice and her role in the poem.[24]

Ross interprets the image used by Prometheus as primarily phallocentric and heterosexual: the male sex act is given precedence and the woman is seen (literally) as the receptacle for male desire. Yet whilst one can see why such an interpretation is possible, one would also want to highlight aspects of the image which, at the same time, work to counter it. The 'overflowing' of Prometheus's 'being' might suggest ejaculation but it is far from suggesting male penetration and, in its uncontrolled and undefined fluidity, hints at a force which, in another context, one might categorise as feminine. The 'chalice', on the other hand, offers a controlling, containing and defining limit to Prometheus's excess and, as such, indicates qualities which might be viewed as masculine. Whilst not deploying gender co-ordinates at this stage in his argument, Jerrold E. Hogle finds the image contained in this speech far more positive than does Ross. Hogle notes that Asia must reflect back to Prometheus the 'self-transcendence' that he has achieved in his retraction of the curse in Act I: 'Otherwise he cannot fully be again the becoming-self-by-becoming-different that he used to be when his "being overflowed" into her "chalice" and was there reshaped (born again) each time they made love.'[25] Hogle interprets this speech as one which challenges rather than consolidates a masculine sense of an autonomous 'self': in his relationship with Asia, Prometheus learns to become 'different' because his being is moulded and shaped by her feminine presence.

Perhaps the challenge offered by Prometheus's speech, and, paradigmatically, the poem as a whole, is not that one has ultimately to accept Ross's reading or that of Hogle but, rather, that one is aware of the co-existence of two apparently opposing interpretations, that one is aware, in short, of the existence of paradox. *Prometheus Unbound* presents the reader with a feminised hero and a masculinised heroine who possess a heterosexual relationship which, whilst based upon the premiss of gender difference, can be seen both to support and subvert patriarchal expectations. Prometheus's speech can be read at a further, metatextual, level to indicate the relationship between poet and text, particularly in relation to genre and the issue of poetic originality. Richard Cronin relates the use of genre to that of a 'mould': 'a genre, like a mould, shapes what it contains, … the genre a poet chooses is not a container in which his meaning is encapsulated, but a part of the meaning.'[26] The 'chalice' in Prometheus's speech is analogous to this generic 'mould' and the 'overflowing' nature of the Titan's 'being' can be related to the poetic spirit as, for example, described by Wordsworth in the 'Preface' to *Lyrical Ballads* as 'the spontaneous overflow of powerful feelings'.[27] The ambiguities and oppositions already discussed in the speech map directly on to the issues raised at this metatextual level: is Shelley implicitly asserting the primacy of a poet's individual imaginative (masculine) originality? Or is he indicating an awareness (and acceptance) of the shaping and controlling force of poetic tradition and precedent? The paradoxical speech yields no ready answers and returns the reader to the paradoxical statement contained in the 'Preface' – that the male poet is both the 'creator' and the 'creation' of the age in which he lives, or that, to use the terms cited by Jerrold Hogle, he cannot achieve a sense of (original) 'self' without also becoming 'different' from and other than that self.

## III

In her definition of 'paradox' which has so far provided a useful point of entry for the present discussion of *Prometheus Unbound*, Isobel Armstrong observes that the 'language' of paradox is one which is involved in 'discovering the void' which exists outside and beyond it. In furthering an exploration of Shelley's analysis of 'difference' within the poem, this notion of a 'void' or emptiness outside of language is one which needs to be pursued, particularly as it is a recurrent implicit theme in much of Shelley's own philosophical speculations. In the essay 'On Life', for example, he describes how it is the aim of Philosophy to act as a 'pioneer' clearing the way for social improvement:

It makes one step towards this object; it destroys error, and the roots of error. It leaves, what is too often the duty of the reformer in political and ethical questions to leave, a vacancy. It reduces the mind to that freedom in which it would have acted, but for the misuse of words and signs, the instruments of its own creation. – By signs, I would be understood in a wide sense, including what is properly meant by that term, and what I peculiarly mean. In this latter sense almost all familiar objects are signs, standing not for themselves but for others, in their capacity of suggesting one thought, which shall lead to a train of thoughts. – Our whole life is thus an education in error.[28]

Shelley's use of the term 'signs' here is extremely broad, suggesting what today one might call all semiotic systems, and he is particularly alert to the ideological function of such systems, of how one 'sign' is dependent upon (suggests or leads to) another. Like Cixous's system of binary oppositions which can all be ultimately mapped on to the hierarchical opposition of 'man/woman', Shelley's signs function as a means of perpetuating 'error', and it is, so he argues, the function of philosophy to destroy the 'roots' of such erroneous thought. What is interesting, however, is that Shelley maintains that the eradication of such error can only, at least in the first instance, lead to a sense of 'vacancy'. If, as Cixous asserts, all discourse within western culture is based upon binary opposition and rigidly defined difference, then one could extrapolate from this that the removal of these binaries can likewise only lead to a vacancy or void. If language, in its largest sense, is 'an education of error' because it is implicated in a repressive ideology, the removal of language will constitute a 'freedom' of sorts, but it will only be a freedom which has no voice with which to express itself.

In *Prometheus Unbound*, Prometheus claims that there is no 'hope' other than that to be found in 'love', and it is to Shelley's essay 'On Love' (1818) that one can turn in order to approach a solution to the problem posed by the essay 'On Life'. For Shelley, love is a force which comes into being with an awareness of lack or vacancy: 'It is that powerful attraction towards all that we conceive or fear or hope beyond ourselves when we find within our own thoughts the chasm of an insufficient void and seek to awaken in all things that are, a community with that we experience in ourselves.'[29] Love, when it is conceived in this way, is concerned with both self and 'community', it is about both self-definition and the interrelationship between self and other. The self is, paradoxically, portrayed as both 'insufficient' and devoid of adequate identity on the one hand, and, on the other, as a presence which has sufficient autonomy to act upon others and communicate 'what we experience in ourselves'. Love is not perceived as either masculine self-assertion or feminine passivity and self-effacement but as a harmonious combination of the two. Love is, furthermore, presented as the fundamental drive and dynamic of life: 'So soon as this want or power is dead, man becomes the living sepulchre of himself, and what survives is the mere husk of what once he was.'[30] Love is both an active 'power' and a recognition of inadequacy, a 'want', but it is crucial to Shelley's purpose that it is the 'want' that creates the 'power' and vice versa. In *Prometheus Unbound*, love, or desire, is the positive response to the vacancy left by the defeat of 'error', a response which is worked towards by Asia in the central sections of the poem.

Before Asia's discovery of the full force of love, however, Shelley reminds the reader of the sterility of human relationships which are based upon binary oppositions and the establishment of rigid difference. Many critics have observed how Prometheus's behaviour at the beginning of the first act mirrors the oppressive nature of Jupiter his enemy and have noted how there is a syntactical elision between the two figures in the first speech. Prometheus notes how Jupiter has inflicted pain and suffering on mankind:

> Whilst me, who am thy foe, eyeless in hate,
> Hast thou made reign and triumph, to thy scorn,
> O'er mine own misery and thy vain revenge. (I.9–11)

The description 'eyeless in hate' applies ironically to both Prometheus and Jupiter, and the vocabulary of triumph and kingship, when applied to Prometheus, equally alerts the reader to potential parallels between the two protagonists. Barbara Charlesworth Gelpi uses these similarities as a starting point to make larger generalisations about the significance of this relationship:

Allusions to the Oedipal story, sprinkled as they are at key points throughout the action of *Prometheus Unbound*, suggest that the two dramas enact a similar interior journey. Act one of *Prometheus Unbound* – where the phrase 'eyeless in hate' (I.i.9) has ambiguous reference to both Jupiter and Prometheus – like one part of the Oedipus cycle describes the tragic conflict with the father produced by the mirroring nature of desire. All male relationships involve a struggle for power, in which language is a false and tyrannical instrument given its fullest expression in a curse.[31]

In this early section of the play, Jupiter attempts to assert his own sense of a masculine self in opposition to that of Jupiter: the result is a self-defeating clash of other-denying masculinity where both men ironically reflect one another in attempting to register their own separate identities. As Gelpi demonstrates, language in this situation becomes a 'curse' (rejecting, cursing the existence of others) and is thus 'a false and tyrannical instrument' analogous to Shelley's account in the essay 'On Life' of 'the misuse of words and signs, the instruments of [the mind's] own creation'. In her pursuit of an understanding of love and desire, Asia needs to discover a language which is free from such 'misuse' and, in doing so, she needs to go beyond, or behind, the self-perpetuating self-destructiveness of the 'Oedipus cycle' as presented by Gelpi.[32]

Asia follows the vision offered by Panthea's dream and is led down into the cave of the mysterious Demogorgon. Moving back to an earlier stage than that represented by the Oedipal scenario, she descends into what becomes a figurative depiction of the maternal womb, a return to a time before corrupted and corrupting language – her song at the end of the act registering the return to an earlier state of innocence that she has been able to achieve:

> We have past Age's icy caves,
> And Manhood's dark and tossing waves
> And Youth's smooth ocean, smiling to betray;
> Beyond the glassy gulphs we flee
> Of shadow-peopled Infancy
> Through Death and Birth to a diviner day. (II.v.98–103)

In the womb-like cave of Demogorgon, Asia discovers 'a mighty Darkness / Filling the seat of Power' (II.iv.2-3), a genderless force whom she proceeds to question about the world she lives in and the power relationships that exist within it. Demogorgon remains cryptic in its responses, constantly turning the tables on its questioner and forcing her to answer her own questions, and, at II.iv.32ff, effectively encouraging her to narrate her own history of the creation of the world and the events which have led to her present situation and that of Prometheus. This control over her own narrative empowers Asia, but the crux of this question-and-answer session comes when she demands of Demogorgon, 'Who is the master of the slave?':

> DEMOGORGON
>                     – If the Abysm
> Could vomit forth its secrets: – but a voice
> Is wanting, the deep truth is imageless;
> For what would it avail to bid thee gaze
> On the revolving world? what to bid speak
> Fate, Time, Occasion, Chance and Change? To these
> All things are subject but eternal Love.

> ASIA
> So much I asked before, and my heart gave
> The response thou hast given; and of such truths
> Each to itself must be the oracle. –
> One more demand ... and do thou answer me
> As my own soul would answer, did it know
> That which I ask. – Prometheus shall arise
> Henceforth the Sun of this rejoicing world:
> When shall the destined hour arrive?
>
> DEMOGORGON
> Behold! (II.iv.114–28)

Having retold her own narrative, Asia has, in effect, removed the 'error' that Shelley writes of in the essay 'On Life' but, having done so, she is left confronting the 'vacancy' that remains: Demogorgon presents her with an 'Abysm' and a 'truth' which is 'imageless' because a 'voice' is 'wanting'. Again, 'Love' would seem to offer some kind of dynamic which would lead beyond this apparent *impasse* and it is implicitly in terms of love, specifically 'love' as it is envisaged in Shelley's essay on the topic, that the scene, and the poem as a whole, is able to progress. Asia comes to realise, in part as a result of her earlier interactions with Demogorgon, that 'Each to itself must be the oracle', that is, that each person must be responsible for their own construction of 'reality'. This is, of course, in keeping with Shelley's belief, expressed in the essay 'On Life', that 'nothing exists but as it is perceived'. None the less, Asia's speech pushes beyond this simple formulation. Despite what she has just said, she proceeds to ask Demogorgon for a response to one more question, asking him to answer 'as [her] own soul would answer'. Implicit in Asia's request is an acknowledgement that her sense of self and self-knowledge is dependent upon the existence of an other and that her question must be moulded into an answer in the 'chalice' of another's understanding before true knowledge can be obtained. The question, when phrased in this 'loving' way becomes, effectively, its own answer and Demogorgon has only to invite her to 'behold' the 'Hours' which brings with it the fall of Jupiter's tyranny and the liberation of Prometheus.

In the cave of Demogorgon Asia discovers a sense of difference which is playful and constantly shifting in contrast to the rigid system of difference and binary opposition that Prometheus learns to reject in Act I; she discovers not 'difference' but Derridean *différance*.

The freed Prometheus announces in Act III that he and the other vic-
torious will retire to a 'Cave' and explore and develop the renewed
'innocence' that Asia discovered in the other 'Cave' of Demogorgon:

> We will entangle buds and flowers, and beams
> Which twinkle on the fountain's brim, and make
> Strange combinations out of common things
> Like human babes in their brief innocence;
> And we will search, with looks and words of love
> For hidden thoughts each lovelier that the last,
> Our unexhausted spirits, and like lutes
> Touched by the skill of the enamoured wind,
> Weave harmonies divine, yet ever new,
> From difference sweet where discord cannot be. (III.iii.30–9)

Such a vision could have marked the end of *Prometheus Unbound*, but
Shelley continued the poem beyond the end of Act III into the lyric
effusions of Act IV. Engaged in this new form of interrelationship –
where, although 'difference' is maintained, it is also constantly in a
state of flux, finding and re-finding itself in the 'other' – the notion
of 'character' becomes redundant for, as Shelley remarks in the essay
'On Life':

The words, *I*, and *you*, and *they*, are grammatical devices invented simply
for arrangement and totally devoid of the intense and exclusive sense
usually attached to them. It is difficult to find terms adequately to
express so subtle a conception as that to which the intellectual philosophy has conducted us. We are on that verge where words abandon us,
and what little wonder if we grow dizzy to look down the dark abyss of
– how little we know.[33]

In *Prometheus Unbound*, however, this 'abyss' has been overcome, as
has been seen, and the poem is able to jettison the false distinctions
offered by '*I*, and *you*, and *they*' through its modulation into a lyrical
outpouring in the final act. Prometheus and the others become
unnecessary presences because all rigid notions of the masculine 'self'
have been lost in a fluid interchange of harmonious 'difference', a
shift which is registered generically through the gradual modulation
from drama into lyric.

It was noted earlier how Shelley's project in *Prometheus Unbound*
could be interpreted as one which attempts to find a way beyond the
sterile hierarchised and gendered binary oppositions described by
Hélène Cixous in 'Sorties'. In his exploration of difference and the
necessary dynamics of 'love' and desire, he approaches a solution

which coincides with that of Cixous herself. Cixous locates hope in the creative forces within society, those forces whom Shelley describes in *A Defence of Poetry* as its 'unacknowledged legislators'.[34] Cixous claims that

> there is no invention possible, whether it be philosophical or poetic, without the presence in the inventing subject of an abundance of the other, of the diverse ... there is no invention of other I's, no poetry, no fiction without a certain homosexuality (interplay therefore of bisexuality) making in me a crystallized work of my ultrasubjectivities. I in this matter, personal, exuberant, lively masculine, feminine, or other in which I delights me and distresses me.[35]

*Prometheus Unbound* overcomes the 'distress' and celebrates the 'delight' that this kind of interrelationship offers, providing as it does so a model for the re-establishment of gender difference whilst at the same time avoiding the injustice and inequality that such difference has often promoted.

## NOTES

1 *London Magazine*, June 1820; quoted in Theodore Redpath (ed.), *The Young Romantics and Critical Opinion*, p.350.

2 Perhaps the best discussion of the genre of *Prometheus Unbound* is that by Stuart Curran in his *Poetic Form and British Romanticism*, pp.198–203; amongst other useful explorations of the topic see, for example, that of Angela Leighton in *Shelley and the Sublime*, pp.75–7.

3 *Quarterly Review*, October 1821 (published December); reprinted in Redpath (ed.), *The Young Romantics*, p.367.

4 For an interesting discussion of the significance of the word 'recall' in this context, see Carol Jacobs, *Uncontainable Romanticism*, pp.25–9. She writes, for example, that '[n]ot only is recall a word that performs the dissemination of its varied meanings, these meanings oddly recapitulate some of our most treasured (if mutually exclusive) theories about how language functions – as a making present in full restoration of that which it names, or as bringing to mind of that which it nevertheless recognises as past, or as that which annuls that of which it speaks' (p.27).

5 Curran, *Poetic Form*, p.199.

6 Richard Cronin, *Shelley's Poetic Thoughts*, p.33.

7 Wordsworth, 'Preface and Appendix to *Lyrical Ballads* 1800, 1802', in *Wordsworth's Literary Criticism*, p.70.

8 Wordsworth, 'Preface', p.69.

9 Wordsworth, 'Preface', p.73.

10 All references to Shelley's poetry and prose are taken from *Shelley's Poetry and Prose* (ed. Reiman and Powers).

11 'On Life', p.476.

12 'On Life', p.477.
13 Cronin, *Shelley's Poetic Thoughts*, p.33.
14 Cronin, *Shelley's Poetic Thoughts*, p.165.
15 Isobel Armstrong, *Language as Living Form in Nineteenth-Century Poetry*, pp.134–5.
16 Hélène Cixous, 'Sorties', in David Lodge (ed.), *Modern Criticism and Theory*, p.287.
17 Marlon B. Ross, *The Contours of Masculine Desire: Romanticism and the Rise of Women's Poetry*, p.139.
18 Timothy Webb, amongst others, notes the Christian precedent for Shelley's location of 'strength' in 'weakness'; see Timothy Webb, *Shelley: A Voice Not Understood*, p.173.
19 Laura Mulvey, 'Visual Pleasure and Narrative Cinema', p.11.
20 Mulvey, 'Visual Pleasure', p.12.
21 For an alternative, but related, discussion of this 'gaze' in relation to gender, see Barbara Charlesworth Gelpi, *Shelley's Goddess*, pp.187–8.
22 Cronin, *Shelley's Poetic Thoughts*, p.147.
23 Marlon B. Ross, *The Contours of Masculine Desire*, p.145.
24 Ross, *The Contours of Masculine Desire*, p.145.
25 Jerrold E. Hogle, *Shelley's Process*, p.180.
26 Cronin, *Shelley's Poetic Thoughts*, p.36.
27 Wordsworth, 'Preface', p.85.
28 Shelley, 'On Life', p.477.
29 Shelley, 'On Love', p.473.
30 Shelley, 'On Love', p.474.
31 Gelpi, *Shelley's Goddess*, pp.203–4.
32 For a version of Asia's quest which is similar to, but distinct from, that presented in the present book, see Gelpi's own analysis in *Shelley's Goddess*, especially pp.170–229.
33 Shelley, 'On Life', p.478. Richard Cronin, following a similar line of enquiry, makes the point that 'Shelley forces the play's reader to engage the paradox that to liberate the individual is also to annihilate him' (*Shelley's Poetic Thoughts*, p.162).
34 Shelley, *A Defence of Poetry*, p.508.
35 Hélène Cixous, 'Sorties', p.292. In this connection, note also Jerrold Hogle's remark that Shelley's 'self-reproducing and self-altering transference is the otherness-of-self-from-self long consigned to "woman" by patriarchal discourse and recently revived in French theory as the feminine "unconscious" on which the construct "man" (including the Freudian version) is actually based without realizing the fact.' (*Shelley's Process*, p.18).

# Conclusion

Recent essays on writing from the 'Romantic Period' have often been grouped together in volumes which gesture in their titles to the current transitional status of Romantic studies. One such collection, for example, proclaims itself to be *At the Limits of Romanticism*, whilst another, perhaps more seemingly adventurous, declares itself to be *Beyond Romanticism*.[1] The editors are, of course, fully aware of the implications and ironies of their titles: both books lay claim to a departure from the study of Romanticism in conventional terms (or, at least, to a new focus on topics which traditional studies of Romanticism have marginalised in favour of the canonical male 'Big Six') and yet the titles simultaneously evoke the very thing that they attempt either to depart from or to redefine. The powerful narrative of Romanticism appears to subvert such attempts to redirect our critical attention towards other literary (and non-literary) productions of the same historical period. Even as these books prepare to move away from an aesthetic and critical hegemony they are forced to confront its lingering dominance and, to adapt Derrida on genre, the title or sign which 'marks' them as belonging to a specific critical undertaking also ironically 'unmarks' them simultaneously. It is, as Derrida says, 'a certain participation without belonging – a taking part in without being part of, without having membership in a set'.[2]

The editors of *Beyond Romanticism* situate themselves critically by drawing the reader's attention to this critical double-bind; they note that:

Romantic criticism continues its struggle simultaneously to define and be rid of itself, a doubleness symptomatic of the continuing dialectical relationship between Romantic construction and Romantic critique. Even the most flamboyant new voices in the recent debate continue to wrestle with a definition of 'the Romantic' at the same time as claiming to have found a way out of its ideology.[3]

As we saw in the Introduction, the notion of such an 'ideology' is a development of the work of Jerome McGann, and our contemporary critical concern to move beyond Romanticism is to a greater or lesser extent a result of ideas stemming from his influential book *The*

*Romantic Ideology*. Yet, as McGann's subsequent pronouncements have made clear, it would be wrong to interpret this Romantic 'ideology' as being monolithic or prescriptive in its tendencies. Whilst we should recognise the force of Romantic narratives, we should also keep in mind McGann's sense of the dynamic nature of Romantic texts. In a later essay, he observes that

> to the extent that romanticism is executed not as a prescriptive but as a poetical economy – a dynamic scene of evolving tensions and relationships, as in a family – its primal terms and data cannot lapse into schematic rectitude. Romantic poetry, in short, constructs a theater for the conflicts and interactions of the ideologies of romanticism.[4]

Not 'ideology', then, but 'ideologies': following McGann's model, the work of the Romantic poets can be read in order to discover conflict and debate rather than other-excluding closure. The readings of a range of Romantic poems that I have offered in the pages of the present book hopefully demonstrate this and show the extent to which Romantic texts frequently challenge what has been reductively thought of as their singular 'ideology'. Even feminist critical strategies can, as has been seen, find a corroborating presence within these poems, even if it is a presence which at times exists precariously alongside more overtly patriarchal tendencies. I would want to agree, therefore, with Julie Ellison's delineation of the relationship between Romanticism and feminism and would extend her focus on Romantic 'criticism' to include the poetry as well:

> Feminist theory has exhibited sustained dislike for the romantic. Nonetheless, feminism and romanticism share an anxiety about aggression and violence; a critique of authority; a commitment to the cognitive validity of feeling and atmosphere; an identification with the victim; an intrigue with the construction and deconstruction of subjectivity. Both psychoanalysis and Marxism, the most prestigious influences within feminist theory, have a romantic prehistory that is powerfully revised but not negated by feminist thinkers. Given this large and endlessly disptutable common ground, can one say that feminism is not romantic? Or that a feminist ethics is not descended from the gendered figurations of romantic criticism?[5]

As Ellison points out, of course, the relationships between feminism and both psychoanalysis and Marxism are far from easy, and there have been as many disagreements as points of contact.[6] The same must necessarily be true of the relationship between feminism and

Romanticism. All those elements which Ellison suggests Romanticism shares with feminism are also challenged in Romantic poetry by what could be seen as their opposites: an anxiety concerning aggression is often matched by aggressive self-assertion; a critique of authority is frequently accompanied by a desire for control; an awareness of the power of 'feeling' is commonly presented alongside an emphasis upon the self-defining power of the mind, and so on. Yet, for all this, I would suggest that Ellison's point still holds; that there is a crucial sympathy between feminism and the 'gendered figurations of romantic criticism' and poetry. Marjorie Levinson has written, perhaps rather cryptically, that 'We are the ones who, by putting the past to a certain use, put it in a certain order. While most of us know this, we seem not to consider this interest of ours in a certain use might also be an *effect* of the past which we study.'[7] Feminism appears as a useful critical strategy for opening up the apparent closure of the Romantic Ideology and yet, as Ellison claims, that very strategy can be viewed as a product of the very thing it would oppose. Feminist strategies are implicitly the 'effect' of the poems upon which they are deployed because these poems foreground those issues of gender, self and society which are central to any feminist enquiry.

Jerome McGann writes of Romantic poetry being a 'theater for the conflicts and interactions of the ideologies of romanticism.' The second half of the present book has focused more literally upon the theatrical aspects of Romanticism: *Otho the Great*, *Manfred* and *Prometheus Unbound* all engage with issues of dramatic performance and gesture in different ways towards the performative nature of gender difference. More generally, however, I would argue, with McGann, for the paradigmatic status of the image of the theatre within Romantic poetry. The theatre is a site for the dramatic interchange of different voices in front of an audience which changes with every performance; the drama is a form which resists easy closure and constantly reminds us of its provisional nature.[8] This I would suggest is how we should attempt to read Romantic poetry, and it is this kind of reading which is aided by an awareness of the role played by genre within a specific text. Genres, to continue the theatrical metaphor, are effectively performed within a poem and that performance is always carried out in a dramatic relationship with other genres which, as we have seen again and again throughout the course of this book, invariably bring with them a variety of gendered inflections. In rediscovering the theatrical nature of Romantic poetry, both in terms of gender and genre, we begin to perceive once more a liberating potential within, rather than beyond, Romanticism.

## NOTES

1 See Favret and Watson (eds), *At the Limits of Romanticism* (1994) and Copley and Whale (eds), *Beyond Romanticism* (1992). Other collections which suggest in their titles a contemporary upheaval in Romantic studies include Johnston et al. (eds), *Romantic Revolutions* (1990) and Martin and Jarvis (eds), *Reviewing Romanticism* (1992).

2 Derrida, 'The Law of Genre', in *Acts of Literature*, p.227.

3 Copley and Whale, *Beyond Romanticism*, p.4; for a subsequent 'flamboyant' voice that implicitly attempts to conflate the difference between 'construction' and 'critique', and thereby posits a newly subversive form of 'Romanticism', see Jerome Christensen, 'The Romantic Movement at the End of History'.

4 McGann, 'Rethinking Romanticism', p.739.

5 Ellison, *Delicate Subjects*, p.11. However, one should also keep in mind Copley and Whale's observation that materialist critiques of Romanticism are always finding that the histories they bring to it are always already part of its substance: 'Slavery, bodies, ruins, revolution and political economy can be seen as the very things which provide the springboard for ... Romantic transcendence, and are thereby included in the very fabric of its idealizing power' (*Beyond Romanticism*, p.7).

6 On the relationship between feminism and Freudian psychoanalysis see, famously, Juliet Mitchell, *Psychoanalysis and Feminism*; for a feminist criticism that combines Marxism and psychoanalysis, see the work of Cora Kaplan in, for example, *Sea Changes*.

7 Levinson, 'The New Historicism: Back to the Future', in *Rethinking Historicism*, p.21.

8 See, in this respect, Don Bialostosky's programme for a 'dialogic' Romantic criticism. However, one should also take heed of Paul Hamilton's reservations concerning the potentially conservative nature of this kind of approach (see Hamilton, 'Wordsworth and the Shapes of Theory').

# Bibliography

Abrams, M.H., *The Mirror and the Lamp: Romantic Theory and the Critical Tradition*, New York and London, Norton, 1958.

Abrams, M.H., 'English Romanticism: The Spirit of the Age' (1963), in *The Correspondent Breeze*.

Abrams, M.H., 'Structure and Style in the Greater Romantic Lyric' (1965), in *The Correspondent Breeze*.

Abrams, M.H., *The Correspondent Breeze: Essays on English Romanticism*, New York and London, Norton, 1984.

Aers, D., Cook, J. and Punter, D., *Romanticism and Ideology: Studies in English Writing 1765–1830*, London, Routledge and Kegan Paul, 1981.

Alexander, M., *Women in Romanticism: Mary Wollstonecraft, Dorothy Wordsworth and Mary Shelley*, London, Macmillan, 1989.

Armstrong, I., *Language as Living Form in Nineteenth-Century Poetry*, Brighton, Harvester, 1982.

Armstrong, I., 'So what's all this about the mother's body?: The Aesthetic, Gender and the Polis', in *Textuality and Sexuality*, ed. Still and Worton.

Barker-Benfield, G.J., *The Culture of Sensibility: Sex and Society in Eighteenth-Century Britain*, Chicago and London, University of Chicago Press, 1992.

Barnard, J., *John Keats*, Cambridge, Cambridge University Press, 1987.

Barrell, J., *Poetry, Language and Politics*, Manchester, Manchester University Press, 1988.

Bate, J., *Shakespeare and the English Romantic Imagination*, Oxford, Clarendon Press, 1989.

Bate, W.J., *John Keats*, Cambridge, Mass., The Belknap Press of Harvard University Press, 1963.

Bennett, Andrew, *Keats, Narrative and Audience: The Posthumous Life of Writing*, Cambridge, Cambridge University Press, 1994.

Bewell, A., 'Keats's Realm of Flora', *Studies in Romanticism*, 31 (spring 1992), 71–98.

Bialostosky, D.H., *Wordsworth, Dialogics, and the Practice of Criticism*, Cambridge, Cambridge University Press, 1992.

Bloom, H., *The Anxiety of Influence: A Theory of Poetry*, Oxford and New York, Oxford University Press, 1973.

Bloom, H. *The Western Canon: The Books and the School of Ages*, London, Macmillan, 1995.

Bloom, H. et al. (eds), *Deconstruction and Criticism*, New York, Seabury, 1979.

Bourke, R., *Romantic Discourse and Political Modernity: Wordsworth, the Intellectual and Cultural Critique*, New York and London, Harvester Wheatsheaf, 1993.

Breen, J. (ed.), *Women Romantic Poets 1785–1832: An Anthology*, London,

Dent and Sons, 1992.

Brigham, L.C., 'The Postmodern Semiotics of *Prometheus Unbound*', *Studies in Romanticism*, 33 (spring 1994), 31–56.

Bromwich, D., *Hazlitt: The Mind of a Critic*, New York and Oxford, Oxford University Press, 1983.

Brown, C.A., *Life of John Keats*, ed. Dorothy Hyde Bodurtha and Willard Bissell Pipe, London and New York, Oxford University Press, 1937.

Burke, E., *A Philosophical Enquiry into the Origins of Our Ideas of the Sublime and the Beautiful*, ed. Adam Phillips, Oxford, Oxford University Press, 1990.

Burroughs, C., 'Acting in the Closet: A Feminist Performance of Hazlitt's *Liber Amoris* and Keats's *Otho the Great*', *European Romantic Review*, 2.2 (1992), 125–44.

Burwick, F. *Illusion and the Drama: Critical Theory of the Enlightenment and Romantic Era*, Philadelphia, Pennsylvania State University Press, 1991.

Butler, J., 'Performative Acts and Gender Constitution: An Essay in Phenomenology and Feminist Theory', in *Performing Feminisms*, ed. Case.

Butler, J., *Gender Trouble: Feminism and the Subversion of Identity*, London, Routledge, 1990.

Butler, M., *Romantics, Rebels and Reactionaries: English Literature and its Background 1760–1830*, Oxford, Oxford University Press, 1981.

Byron, G., *Byron's Letters and Journals*, ed. Leslie A Marchand, 12 volumes, Cambridge, Mass., Harvard University Press, 1973–82.

Byron, G., *Poetical Works*, ed. Frederick Page, new edition corrected by John Jump, Oxford, Oxford University Press, 1970.

Carlson, J.A., *In the Theatre of Romanticism: Coleridge, Nationalism, Women*, Cambridge, Cambridge University Press, 1994.

Caruth, C., *Empirical Truths and Critical Fictions: Locke, Wordsworth, Kant, Freud*, Baltimore and London, Johns Hopkins University Press, 1990.

Case, S.-E., *Performing Feminisms: Feminist Critical Theory and Theatre*, Baltimore and London, Johns Hopkins University Press, 1990.

Cave, R.A. (ed.), *The Romantic Theatre: An International Symposium*, Totowa, Barnes and Noble Books, 1986.

Chase, C. (ed.), *Romanticism*, London and New York, Longman, 1993.

Christensen, J., *Lord Byron's Strength: Romantic Writing and Commercial Society*, Baltimore and London, Johns Hopkins University Press, 1993.

Christensen, J., 'The Romantic Movement at the End of History', *Critical Inquiry*, 20 (spring 1994), 452–76.

Cixous, H., 'Sorties', trans. Anne Liddle, in *New French Feminisms*, ed. Marks and de Courtivron.

Cixous, H., 'Castration or Decapitation', trans. Annette Kuhn, *Signs*, 7.1 (1983), 36–55.

Claridge, L., 'The Bifurcated Female Space of Desire: Shelley's Confrontation with Language and Silence', in *Out of Bounds*, ed. Claridge and Langland.

Claridge, L. and Langland, E., *Out of Bounds: Male Writers and Gender(ed) Criticism*, Amherst, University of Massachusetts Press, 1990.

Clark, S. and Worrall D. (eds), *Historicizing Blake*, London, Macmillan, 1994.

Coleridge, S.T., *Poems*, ed. John Beer, London, Dent, revised ed., 1974.

Coleridge, S.T., *Complete Poetical Works*, ed. E.H. Coleridge, Oxford, Oxford University Press, 1912.

Coleridge, S.T., *Selected Letters*, ed. H.J. Jackson, Oxford, Oxford University Press, 1987.

Coleridge. S.T., *Biographia Literaria or Biographical Sketches of My Life and Opinions*, ed. James Engel and W. Jackson Bate, 2 volumes, London and Princeton: Routledge and Kegan Paul, and Princeton University Press, 1983.

Copley, S. and Whale, J. (eds), *Beyond Romanticism: New Approaches to Texts and Contexts 1780–1832*, London, Routledge, 1992.

Cox, J.N. (ed.), *Seven Gothic Dramas 1789–1825*, Athens, Ohio University Press, 1992.

Cox, P., 'Valleys of Seclusion: The Gendered Discourse of Romantic Pastoral', in Höhne (ed.), *Romantic Discourses*.

Cox, P., ' "Among the Flocks of Tharmas": *The Four Zoas* and the Pastoral of Commerce', in Clark and Worrall (eds), *Historicizing Blake*.

Cox, P., ' "Feelings all too delicate for use": Coleridge and the Gendering of Genre', *Journal of Gender Studies*, 4.1 (1995), 27–34.

Cox, P., 'Keats and the Performance of Gender', *Keats–Shelley Journal*, 44 (1995), 24–50.

Cronin, R., *Shelley's Poetic Thoughts*, London, Macmillan, 1981.

Culler, J., 'The Mirror Stage', in *High Romantic Art*, ed. Lipking.

Curran, S., *Poetic Form and British Romanticism*, New York and Oxford, Oxford University Press, 1986.

Curran, S., 'Romantic Poetry: The I Altered', in Mellor (ed.), *Romanticism and Feminism*.

Curran, S., 'Women Readers, Women Writers', in Curran (ed.), *Cambridge Companion*.

Curran, S. (ed.), *The Cambridge Companion to British Romanticism*, Cambridge, Cambridge University Press, 1993.

Davie, D., *Articulate Energy*, London, Routledge and Kegan Paul, 1955.

de Almeida, H. (ed.), *Critical Essays on John Keats*, Boston, G.K. Hall, 1990.

de Bolla, P., *Harold Bloom: Towards Historical Rhetorics*, London and New York, Routledge, 1988.

Derrida, J., 'Living On: Border Lines', trans. James Hulbert, in Harold Bloom et al. (eds), *Deconstruction and Criticism*.

Derrida, J. *Acts of Literature*, ed. Derek Attridge, New York and London, Routledge, 1992.

Dubrow, H., *Genre*, The Critical Idiom, London and New York, Methuen, 1982.

Easthope, A., *Poetry and Phantasy*, Cambridge, Cambridge University Press, 1989.

Ellison, Julie, *Delicate Subjects: Romanticism, Gender, and the Ethics of Understanding*, Ithaca and London, Cornell University Press, 1990.

Everest, K., *Coleridge's Secret Ministry: The Context of the Conversation Poems 1795–1798*, Brighton, Harvester, 1979.

Everest, K. (ed.), *Revolution in Writing: British Literary Responses to the French*

*Revolution*, Milton Keynes and Philadelphia, Open University Press, 1991.

Favret, M.A. and Watson, N.J. (eds), *At the Limits of Romanticism: Essays in Cultural, Feminist, and Materialist Criticism*, Bloomington and Indianapolis, Indiana University Press, 1994.

Ferguson, F., *Solitude and the Sublime: Romanticism and the Aesthetics of Individuation*, New York and London, Routledge, 1992.

Foster, M., ' "Tintern Abbey" and Wordsworth's Scene of Writing', *Studies in Romanticism*, 25 (spring 1986), 75–95.

Foucault, M., *Discipline and Punish*, trans. Alan Sheridan, New York, Vintage Books, 1979.

Freud S., 'On Narcissism: An Introduction', trans Joan Riviere, *Collected Papers*, 4, London, The Hogarth Press, 1957.

Fruman, N., *Coleridge, the Damaged Archangel*, London, George Allen and Unwin, 1971.

Frye, N., *Fearful Symmetry: A Study of William Blake*, Princeton, Princeton University Press, 1947.

Furniss, T., 'Gender in Revolution: Edmund Burke and Mary Wollstonecraft', in *Revolution in Writing*, ed. Everest.

Gelpi, B.C., *Shelley's Goddess: Maternity, Language, Subjectivity*, Oxford and New York, Oxford University Press, 1992.

Gerard, A., 'Clevedon Revisited: Further reflections on Coleridge's "Reflections on having left a place of Retirement"', *Notes and Queries*, New Series 7 (1960), 101–2.

Gilbert, S.M. and Gubar, S., *The Madwoman in the Attic: The Woman Writer and the Nineteenth-Century Literary Imagination*, New Haven and London, Yale University Press, 1979.

Gilbert, S.M. and Gubar, S., ' "But oh! that deep romantic chasm": The Engendering of Periodization', *The Kenyon Review*, 13.3 (1991), 74–81.

Gill, S., *William Wordsworth: A Life*, Oxford, Clarendon Press, 1989.

Gittings, R., *John Keats*, London, Heinemann, 1968.

Hamilton, P., 'Wordsworth and the Shapes of Theory', *News from Nowhere: Theory and Politics of Romanticism* (1995), 11–21.

Hazlitt, W., *The Works of William Hazlitt*, ed. P.P. Howe, 21 volumes, London and Toronto, Dent and Sons, 1930–34.

Heller, J.R., *Coleridge, Lamb, Hazlitt, and the Reader of the Drama*, Columbia and London, University of Missouri Press, 1990.

Hertz, N., *The End of the Line: Essays on Psychoanalysis and the Sublime*, New York, Columbia University Press, 1985.

Hofkosh, S., 'A Woman's Profession: Sexual Difference and the Romance of Authorship', *Studies in Romanticism*, 32 (summer 1993), 245–72.

Hogle, J.E., *Shelley's Process: Radical Transference and the Development of His Major Works*, New York and Oxford, Oxford University Press, 1988.

Höhne, H. (ed.), *Romantic Discourses*, Studien zur Englischen Romantik, Essen, Die Blaue Eule, 1994.

Holmes, R., *Coleridge: Early Visions*, London, Hodder and Stoughton, 1989.

Homans, M., *Women Writers and Poetic Identity: Dorothy Wordsworth, Emily Bronte and Emily Dickinson*, Princeton, Princeton University Press, 1980.

Homans, M. 'Keats Reading Women, Women Reading Keats', *Studies in Romanticism*, 29 (fall 1990), 341–70.

Hošek, C. and Parker, P. (eds), *Lyric Poetry: Beyond New Criticism*, Ithaca and London, Cornell University Press, 1985.

Howells, C.A., *Love, Mystery, and Misery: Feeling in Gothic Fiction*, London, The Athlone Press, 1978.

Jacobs, C., *Uncontainable Romanticism. Shelley, Bronte, Kleist*, Baltimore and London, Johns Hopkins University Press, 1989.

Jacobus, M., *Tradition and Experiment in Wordsworth's 'Lyrical Ballads'* (1798), Oxford, Clarendon Press, 1976.

Jacobus, M., *Romanticism, Writing, and Sexual Difference: Essays on 'The Prelude'*, Oxford, Clarendon Press, 1989.

Jarvis, R., *Wordsworth, Milton, and the Theory of Poetic Relations*, London, Macmillan, 1991.

Johnston, K. et al. (eds), *Romantic Revolutions: Criticism and Theory*, Bloomington and Indianapolis, Indiana University Press, 1990.

Jones, C., 'Radical Sensibility in the 1790s', in Yarrington and Everest (eds), *Reflections of Revolution*.

Jones, C., *Radical Sensibility: Literature and Ideas in the 1790s*, London and New York, Routledge, 1993.

Jones, M., 'Double Economics: Ambivalence in Wordsworth's Pastoral', *PMLA*, 108.5 (1993), 1098–113.

Kabitogou, E.D., 'Problematics of Gender in the Nuptials of *The Prelude*', *The Wordsworth Circle*, 19 (1988), 128–35.

Kaplan, C., *Sea Changes: Culture and Feminism*, London, Verso, 1986.

Keats, J., *The Poems of John Keats*, ed. Miriam Allott, London, Longman, 1970, corrected ed. 1975.

Keats, J., *Letters of John Keats: A New Selection*, ed. Robert Gittings, Oxford and New York, Oxford University Press, 1970.

Kelly, G., 'The Limits of Genre and the Institution of Literature: Between Fact and Fiction', in Johnston et al. (eds), *Romantic Revolutions*.

Kolodny, A., 'A Map for Reading: Gender and the Interpretation of Literary Texts', in Showalter (ed.), *New Feminist Criticism*.

Kramer, L., 'Gender and Sexuality in *The Prelude*: The Question of Book Seven', *ELH*, 54.3 (1987), 619–37.

Kristeva, J., *Desire in Language: A Semiotic Approach to Literature and Art*, ed. Leon S. Roudiez, trans. Thomas Gora, Alice Jardine and Leon S. Roudiez, Oxford, Blackwell, 1981.

Kristeva, J., *Powers of Horror: An Essay on Abjection*, trans. Leon S. Roudiez, New York, Columbia University Press, 1982.

Kristeva, J. *The Kristeva Reader*, ed. Toril Moi, Oxford Blackwell, 1986.

Labbe, J.M., Review of Mellor, A.K., *Romanticism and Gender, The Wordsworth Circle*, 25.4 (1994), 261–3.

Lamb, C., *Lamb as Critic*, ed. Roy Park, London and Henley, Routledge and Kegan Paul, 1980.

Leighton, A., *Shelley and the Sublime: An Interpretation of the Major Poems*, Cambridge, Cambridge University Press, 1984.

Levinson, M., *Wordsworth's Great Period Poems: Four Essays*, Cambridge, Cambridge University Press, 1986.

Levinson, M., *Keats's Life of Allegory: The Origin of a Style*, Oxford, Blackwell, 1988.

Levinson, M., 'The New Historicism: Back to the Future', in Levinson et al. (eds), *Rethinking Historicism*.

Levinson, M., Butler, M., McGann, J. and Hamilton, P., *Rethinking Historicism: Critical Readings in Romantic History*, Oxford, Blackwell, 1989.

Lipking, L. (ed.), *High Romantic Art: Essays for M.H. Abrams*, Ithaca, Cornell University Press, 1981.

Liu, A., '"Shapeless Eagerness": The Genre of Revolution in Books 9–10 of *The Prelude*', *Modern Language Quarterly*, 43.1 (1982), 3–28.

Lodge, D. (ed.), *Modern Criticism and Theory: A Reader*, London and New York, 1988.

Lonsdale, R. (ed.), *The New Oxford Book of Eighteenth-Century Poetry*, Oxford, Oxford University Press, 1984.

Lonsdale, R. (ed.), *Eighteenth-Century Women Poets*, Oxford, Oxford University Press, 1990.

McFarland, T., *William Wordsworth: Intensity and Achievement*, Oxford, Clarendon Press, 1992.

McGann, J.J., *The Romantic Ideology: A Critical Investigation*, Chicago and London, Chicago University Press, 1983.

McGann, J.J., 'Rethinking Romanticism', *ELH*, 59 (1992), 735–54.

Machin, R. and Norris, C. (eds), *Post-Structuralist Readings of English Poetry*, Cambridge, Cambridge University Press, 1987.

McKeon, M., 'Historicizing Patriarchy: The Emergence of Gender Difference in England 1660–1760', *Eighteenth-Century Studies*, 28.3 (1995), 295–322.

Magnuson, P., *Coleridge and Wordsworth: A Lyrical Dialogue*, Princeton, Princeton University Press, 1988.

Marks, E. and de Courtivron, I. (eds), *New French Feminisms*, Brighton, Harvester, 1980.

Martin, P.W., *Byron: A Poet before his Public*, Cambridge, Cambridge University Press, 1982.

Martin, P.W., 'Romanticism, History, Historicisms', in Everest (ed.), *Revolution in Writing*.

Martin, P.W. and Jarvis, R. (eds), *Reviewing Romanticism*, London, Macmillan, 1992.

Matthews, G.M. (ed.), *Keats: The Critical Heritage*, London and Boston, Routledge and Kegan Paul, 1971.

Mee, J., *Dangerous Enthusiasm: William Blake and the Culture of Radicalism in the 1790s*, Oxford, Clarendon Press, 1992.

Mellor, A.K. (ed.), *Romanticism and Feminism*, Bloomington and Indianapolis, Indiana University Press, 1988.

Mellor, A.K., *Romanticism and Gender*, London, Routledge, 1993.

Metzger, L., *One Foot in Eden: Modes of Pastoral in Romantic Poetry*, Chapel Hill and London, University of North Carolina Press, 1986.

Milton, J., *Paradise Lost*, ed. Alastair Fowler, revised ed., London, Longman, 1971.

Mitchell, K., *Psychoanalysis and Feminism*, Harmondsworth, Penguin, 1975.

Moi, T., *Sexual/Textual Politics: Feminist Literary Theory*, London and New

York, Routledge, 1985.

Moore, J., 'Plagiarism with a Difference: Subjectivity in "Kubla Khan" and *Letters written during a Short Residence in Norway and Denmark*', in Copley and Whale (eds), *Beyond Romanticism*.

Moorman, M., *William Wordsworth: A Biography. The Early Years 1770–1803*, Oxford, Clarendon Press, 1957.

More, H., *Sacred Dramas chiefly intended for Young Persons. The Subjects taken from the Bible*, eleventh ed., London, Cadell, Jr and Davies, 1799.

Mulvey, L. 'Visual Pleasure and Narrative Cinema'. *Screen*, 16 (autumn 1975), 6–18.

Page, J., '"The weight of too much liberty": Gender and Genre in Wordsworth's Calais Sonnets', *Criticism*, 30.2 (1988), 189–203.

Page, J., ' "A History/Homely and Rude": Genre and Style in Wordsworth's "Michael"', *Studies in English Literature 1500–1900*, 29.4 (1989), 621–36.

Park, R., *Hazlitt and the Spirit of the Age: Abstraction and Critical Theory*, Oxford, Clarendon Press, 1971.

Peterfreund, S. '*The Prelude*: Wordsworth's Metamorphic Epic', *Genre*, 14 (1981), 441–72.

Peterfreund, S., 'Dying into Newtonian Time: Wordsworth and the Elegiac Task', *Genre*, 23 (1990), 279–96.

Pocock, J.G.A., *Virtue, Commerce, and History: Essays on Political Thought and History, Chiefly in the Eighteenth Century*, Cambridge, Cambridge University Press, 1985.

Poovey, M., *The Proper Lady and the Woman Writer: Ideology as Style in the Works of Mary Wollstonecraft, Mary Shelley and Jane Austen*, Chicago and London, University of Chicago Press, 1984.

Rajan, T., 'Romanticism and the Death of Lyric Consciousness', in Hošek and Parker (eds), *Lyric Poetry*.

Rajan, T., 'The Erasure of Narrative in Post-Structuralist Representations of Wordsworth', in Johnston et al. (eds), *Romantic Revolutions*.

Rajan, T., *Dark Interpreter: The Discourse of Romanticism*, Ithaca and London, Cornell University Press, 1980.

Rajan, T., *The Supplement of Reading: Figures of Understanding in Romantic Theory and Practice*, Ithaca and London, Cornell University Press, 1990.

Redpath, T. (ed.), *The Young Romantics and Critical Opinion 1807–1824: Poetry of Byron, Shelley, and Keats as seen by their contemporary critics*, London, Harrap, 1973.

Reed, A. (ed.), *Romanticism and Language*, London, Methuen, 1984.

Richardson, A., 'Romanticism and the Colonization of the Feminine', in Mellor (ed.), *Romanticism and Feminism*.

Roe, N., 'Wordsworth, Milton, and the Politics of Poetic Influence', *The Yearbook of English Studies*, 19 (1989), pp.112–26.

Roe, N., 'Keats's Lisping Sedition', *Essays in Criticism*, 42.1 (1992), 36–55.

Roe, N., *The Politics of Nature: Wordsworth and Some Contemporaries*, London, Macmillan, 1992.

Ross, M.B., 'Naturalizing Gender: Woman's Place in Wordsworth's Ideological Landscape', *ELH*, 53 (1986), 391–410.

Ross, M.B., 'Romantic Quest and Conquest – Troping Masculine Power in the Crisis of Poetic Identity', in Mellor (ed.), *Romanticism and Feminism*.

Ross, M.B., *The Contours of Masculine Desire: Romanticism and the Rise of Women's Poetry*, Oxford, Oxford University Press, 1989.

Ross, M.B., ' "Beyond the Fragmented Word": Keats at the Limits of Patrilineal Language', in Claridge and Langland (eds), *Out of Bounds*.

Rzepka, C.J., '*Theatrum Mundi* and Keats's *Otho the Great*: The Self in "Society"', *Romanticism Past and Present*, 8.1 (1984), 35–55.

Salveson, C., 'Hazlitt and Byron – Intermittent Affinities', in Höhne (ed.), *Romantic Discourses*.

Schapiro, B.A., *The Romantic Mother: Narcissistic Patterns in Romantic Poetry*, Baltimore and London, Johns Hopkins University Press, 1983.

Schultz, M.F., 'Coleridge, Milton and Lost Paradise', *Notes and Queries*, New Series 6 (1959), 143–4.

Sekora, J., Luxury: *The Concept In Western Thought, Eden to Smollett*, Baltimore and London, Johns Hopkins University Press, 1977.

Shelley, P.B., *Shelley's Poetry and Prose*, ed. Donald H. Reiman and Sharon B. Powers, New York and London, W.W. Norton and Co., 1977.

Shiach, M., *Hélène Cixous: A Politics of Writing*, London and New York, Routledge, 1991.

Showalter, E., *The New Feminist Criticism: Essays on Women, Literature and Theory*, London, Virago, 1986.

Simpson, D., *Romanticism, Nationalism, and the Revolt Against Theory*, Chicago and London, University of Chicago Press, 1993.

Siskin, C., *The Historicity of Romantic Discourse*, New York and Oxford, Oxford University Press, 1988.

Sitterson, J.C., 'The Genre and Place of the Intimations Ode', *PMLA*, 101.1 (1986), 24–37.

Smith, A., *An Enquiry into the Nature and Causes of the Wealth of Nations*, 3 volumes, fifth ed., London, Strahan, 1789.

Smith, C., *The Poems of Charlotte Smith*, ed. Stuart Curran, New York and Oxford, Oxford University Press, 1993.

Spivak, G.C., 'Sex and History in *The Prelude* (1805) Books IX to XIII', in Machin and Norris (eds), *Post-Structuralist Readings of English Poetry*.

Springer, M., *What Manner of Woman: Essays on English and American Life and Literature*, Oxford, Blackwell, 1977.

Still, J. and Worton, M. (eds), *Textuality and Sexuality: Reading Theories and Practices*, Manchester, Manchester University Press, 1993.

Taylor, I. and Luria, G., 'Gender and Genre: Women in British Romanticism', in Springer (ed.), *What Manner of Woman*.

Todorov, T., *The Fantastic: A Structural Approach to Literary Genre*, trans. Richard Howard, Cleveland, Ohio, Case Western Reserve Press, 1973.

Todorov, T., *Genres in Discourse*, trans. Catherine Porter, Cambridge, Cambridge University Press, 1990.

Vendler, H., *The Odes of John Keats*, Cambridge, Mass., and London, Belknap Press of Harvard University Press, 1983.

Ward, A., *John Keats: The Making of a Poet*, New York, Farrar, Straus and Giroux, 1963, revised ed. 1986.

Watkins, D.P., 'A Reassessment of Keats's *Otho the Great*', *CLIO*, 16.1 (1986), 49–66.

Watkins, D.P., *A Materialist Critique of English Romantic Drama*, Gainesville, University Press of Florida, 1993.

Webb, T., *Shelley: A Voice Not Understood*, Manchester, Manchester University Press, 1977.

Webb, T., 'The Romantic Poet and the Stage: A Short, Sad History', in Cave (ed.), *The Romantic Theatre*.

Weiskel, T., *The Romantic Sublime: Studies in the Structure and Psychology of Transcendence*, Baltimore and London, Johns Hopkins University Press, 1976.

Williams, J., 'Wordsworth's "Tintern Abbey" in Context: Gender, Art and Romanticism', *News From Nowhere: Theory and Politics of Romanticism* (1995), 120–34.

Wolfson, S.J., '"A Problem Few Dare Imitate": *Sardanapalus* and "Effeminate Character"', *ELH*, 58 (1991), 867–902.

Wolfson, S.J., 'Feminizing Keats', in de Almeida (ed.), *Critical Essays on John Keats*.

Wolfson, S.J., Review of Ruoff, G.W., (ed.), *The Romantics and Us: Essays on Literature and Culture* (1990) and Johnston, K.R. et al. (eds), *Romantic Revolutions: Criticism and Theory* (1990), *Studies in Romanticism*, 32 (spring 1993), 119–30.

Wollstonecraft, M., *Vindication of the Rights of Woman*, ed. Miriam Brody, Harmondsworth, Penguin, 1975.

Woodman, R., 'The Androgyne in *Prometheus Unbound*', *Studies in Romanticism*, 20 (spring 1981), 225–47.

Wordsworth, W., *William Wordsworth*, The Oxford Authors, ed. Stephen Gill, Oxford, Oxford University Press, 1984.

Wordsworth, W., *The Prelude 1799, 1805, 1850*, ed. Jonathon Wordsworth, M.H. Abrams and Stephen Gill, New York and London, W.W. Norton and Co., 1979.

Wordsworth, W., *Letters of William Wordsworth*, ed. Alan G. Hill, Oxford, Oxford University Press, 1984.

Wordsworth, W., *Wordsworth's Literary Criticism*, ed. W.J.B. Owen, London and Boston, Routledge and Kegan Paul, 1974.

Yarrington, A. and Everest, K. (eds), *Reflections of Revolution: Images of Romanticism*, London and New York, Routledge, 1993.

Young, R. (ed.), *Untying the Text: A Post-Structuralist Reader*, Boston and London, Routledge and Kegan Paul, 1981.

# Index